Life In The UK test Handbook

(Comic Version)

ACKNOWLEDGEMENT

This book is dedicated to my wife Zaina, she inspired me to write this book, I still remember her sad and depressed face after reading the official handbook, I felt the pain of all the people struggling to give exam due to their language barrier. My book is a simplified version of an official book. The pictures, slides, and color will help you to learn and understand faster. Special thanks to my sister Avni, who conscientiously supported me, Vivek and Shivani, who helped me to bring this book to reality. With this book, you will get the online premium membership for free. I encourage to test your knowledge after finishing each chapter. I tried my best, but English is my second language so I am open for any suggestions.

Good Luck
Adam
Founder of Lifeintheuktest.biz

Life in the UK - Book Contents

6

Applying to become a permanent resident or citizen of the UK is an important decision and commitment. You will be agreeing to accept the responsibilities which go with permanent residence and to respect the laws, values and traditions of the UK. Good citizens are an asset to the UK. We welcome those seeking to make a positive contribution to our society.

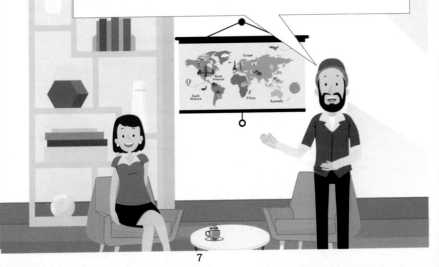

Passing the Life in the UK test is part of demonstrating that you are ready to become a permanent migrant to the UK. This handbook is designed to support you in your preparation. It will help you to integrate into society and play a full role in your local community. It will also help ensure that you a have a broad general knowledge of the culture, laws and history of the UK.

The Life in the UK test is usually taken in English, although special arrangements can be made if you wish to take it in Welsh or Scottish Gaelic.

There are about 60 test centres around the UK. You can only book your test online, at www.lifeintheuktest.gov.uk. You should not take your test at any other establishment as the UK Border Agency will only accept certificates from registered test centres.

You can only take the test at a registered and approved Life in the UK test centre.

If you live on the Isle of Man or in the Channel Islands, there are different arrangements for taking the Life in the UK test.

11

13

16

If I am correct, UK has a pledge too?

Yes. The pledge is as follows 'I will give my loyalty to the United Kingdom and respect its rights and freedom. I will uphold its democratic values. I will observe its law faithfully and fulfil my duties and obligations as a British Citizen.'

Adam how I am going to remember what I have read so far.

Zaina remember the best know quote "Repetition is the mother of learning" read this book few times and practice question for free online www.lifeintheuktest.biz.

Thanks Adam, I will read few times until I feel I have good understanding.

Please pay attention you will see few question, from what I am going to explain you now.

If you wish to be a permanent resident or citizen of the U.K, you should:
- Respect and Obey the laws
- Respect the right of others
- Treat others with fairness
- Look after yourself and your family
- Look after the area in which you live and the environment

In Return, the UK offers to every citizen.
- Freedom of belief and Religion
- Freedom of Speech
- Freedom of unfair discrimination
- A right to a fair trial
- A right to join in the election of a Government.

What do we get in return?

Ok!
So what is the procedure to become a permanent Resident of U.K?

24

Now I have understood everything regarding the principles and the Life in the UK test.

But let me tell you, we are not finished yet. There is a lot more to learn.

Just a simple question, do you know the official name of U.K?

No... !!!

29

The official name is "United Kingdom of Great Britain and Northern Ireland." you will see on british passport

British Passport

The words 'Britain ', 'British Isles' or 'British', however, are used in this book to refer everyone in the UK.

Map

There are also several islands which are closely linked with the UK but are not a part of it e.g the channel islands and the Isle of Man. These have their own governments and are called "Crown Dependencies".

There are also several British overseas territories in other parts of the world, such as St Helena and the Falkland Islands. They are also linked to the UK but are not a part of it.

The UK is governed by the parliament sitting in Westminster. Scotland, Wales and Northern Ireland also have parliaments or assemblies of their own, with devolved powers in defined areas.

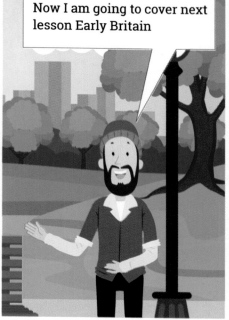

Now I am going to cover next lesson Early Britain

Chapter 3 – A Long and Illustrious History

Houses   Tombs

These people built houses, tombs and monuments on the land. One of these monuments.

Map of Britain Before

Map of Britain After Separation 10,000 Years Ago.

Monuments

The example of this is Stonehenge, still stands in what is now the English country of Wiltshire. Stonehenge was probably a special gathering place for seasonal ceremonies.

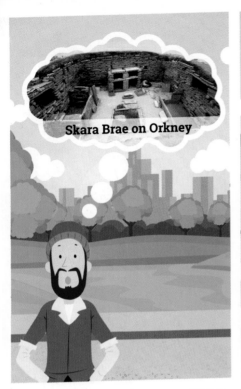

Skara Brae on Orkney

Another good example is Skara Brae on Orkney, off the north coast of Scotland, is the best preserved prehistoric village in northern Europe, and has helped archaeologists to understand more about how people lived near the end of the Stone Age.

Bronze age

What about Bronze age?

Roundhouses

ROUND BARROWS

Around 4,000 years ago, people learned to make bronze. We call this period the Bronze Age. People lived in roundhouses and buried their dead in tombs called Round Barrows.

Ornaments & Weapons

The people of the Bronze Age were accomplished metalworkers who made many beautiful objects.

Maiden Castle, Hill Forts

The Bronze Age was followed by the Iron Age, when people learned how to make weapons and tools out of iron.

First Coins

The people of the Iron Age had a sophisticated culture and economy. Do you know they made the first coins to be minted in Britain. Some coins were inscribed with the names of Iron Age kings. This marks the beginnings of British history.

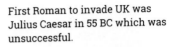

Now I am going to explain very interesting topic which changed the shape of UK " Invasion of Romans"

First Roman to invade UK was Julius Caesar in 55 BC which was unsuccessful.

Claudius

In AD 43 the Roman Army was led by Emperor Claudius in a sally. This time, there was resistance from some of the British tribes but the Romans were successful in occupying almost all of Britain.

Boudicca

One of the tribal leaders who fought against the Romans was Boudicca, the queen of the Iceni in what is now eastern England. She is still remembered today and there is a statue of her on Westminster Bridge in London, near the Houses of Parliament.

HADRIAN

Do you know scotland was never conquered by the Romans, and the Emperor Hadrian built a wall in the north of England to keep out the Picts (ancestors of the Scottish people). Included in the wall were a number of forts. Parts of Hadrian's Wall, including the forts of Housesteads and Vindolanda, can still be seen.
It is a popular area for walkers and is a UNESCO (United Nations Education, Scientific and Cultural Organization)

Here's a list of some of the things the Romans introduced to Britain: The calendar we still use today. The census – the practice of counting a population. High-quality straight roads Central heating Aqueducts (water bridges) Indoor plumbing Towns Cabbages Peas Public libraries Public noticeboards Firemen Police Stinging nettles Cats Grapes Pears Paved streets Turnips Carrots Cement Bricks Heated baths Language (Latin)

The Romans remained in Britain for 400 years. They built roads and public buildings, created a structure of law, and introduced new plants and animals. It was during the 3rd and 4th centuries AD that the first Christian communities began to appear in Britain.

Very interesting...

Yes dear....
Now I will tell you about
Anglo-Saxons.

The Roman army left Britain in AD 410 to defend other parts of the Roman Empire and never returned. Britain was again invaded by tribes from northern Europe: the Jutes, the Angles and the Saxons.

If we use the modern names for the countries they came from, the Saxons, Franks and Frisians were German-Dutch, the Angles were southern Danish, and Jutes were northern Danish.

Ok. And what languages they spoke?

About AD 600, Anglo-Saxon kingdoms were established in Britain. These kingdoms were mainly in what is now England.
These tribes used to speak English.

Parts of the west of Britain, including much of what is now Wales, and Scotland, remained free of Anglo-Saxon rule.

Anglo-Saxons

They buried their King with treasure and armour, placed in a ship which was then covered by a mound of earth: you can see on King burial place at Sutton Hoo, Suffolk.

The Anglo-Saxons were not Christians when they first came to Britain but, during this period, missionaries came to Britain to preach about Christianity. Missionaries from Ireland spread the religion in the north.

St Patrick

Honey, do you know about St Patrick?

Not exactly....

St Patrick, who would become the patron saint of Ireland, and St Columba, who founded a monastery on the island of Iona, off the coast of what is now Scotland.

St Augustine led missionaries from Rome, who spread Christianity in the south. St Augustine became the first Archbishop of Canterbury.

Have you ever heard of Vikings?

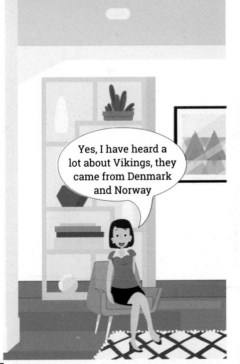

Yes, I have heard a lot about Vikings, they came from Denmark and Norway

The Vikings

True... The Vikings came from Denmark and Norway. **They first visited Britain in AD 789 to raid coastal towns and take away goods and slaves.** Then they began to stay and form their own communities in the east of England and Scotland.

Was there a battle between Anglo-Saxon and Vikings?

Right Zaina. The Anglo-Saxon kingdoms in England united under King Alfred the Great, who defeated the Vikings.

King Alfred
The Great

Many of the Viking invaders stayed in Britain – especially in the east and north of England in an area known as the Danelaw (many place names there, such as Grimsby and Scunthorpe come from the Viking languages). The Viking settlers mixed with local communities and some converted to Christianity.

Who was Kenneth MacAlpin?

In the north, the threat of attack by Vikings had encouraged the people to unite under one king, Kenneth MacAlpin. The term Scotland began to be used to describe that country.

Now I am going to tell you about Norman Conquest.

Hmm... Okay.

In 1066, William, the Duke of Normandy, invaded the England and defeated Harold, the Saxon king of England.

William

Harold was killed in the Battle of Hastings, and he became the king of England and he was known as "William the Conqueror".

Harold

Bayeux Tapestry

The battle is commemorated in a great piece of embroidery, known as the Bayeux tapestry, which can still be seen in France today.

Honey, how long is the Bayeux tapestry?

Dear, Bayeux Tapestry - the linen cloth is nearly 70 metres (230 feet) long and is embroidered with coloured wool

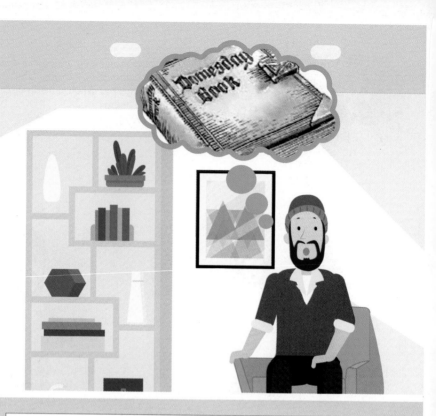

William sent people all over England to draw up lists of all the towns and villages. The people who lived there, who owned the land and what animals they owned were also listed. This was called the Domesday Book. It still exists today and gives a picture of society in England just after the Norman Conquest.

Honey I must say, the way you teach, History seems so easy.

Oh... Really.
Then tell me, who built the Tower of London?

I know... I know...
The Tower of London was built by William the Conqueror after he became King in 1066.

Haha... that's a right answer.

Now let's start the next topic "War at Home and abroad".

War at Home and abroad?

Norman Conquest

The period after the Norman Conquest up until about 1485 is called the Middle Ages (or the medieval period). It was a time of almost constant war.
The English kings fought with the Welsh, Scottish and Irish noblemen for control of their lands.

King Edward I

In 1284 King Edward I of established their rule in Wales, Edward introduced the "Statute of Rhuddlan"
Statute = (a written law)
Rhuddlan = (is a town in Wales)
which annexed = (to attach) Wales to the Crown of England.

By the middle of the 15th century the last Welsh rebellions had been defeated. English laws and the English language were introduced.

Wow that's really fascinating.

Robert the Bruce

In 1314 the Scottish, led by Robert the Bruce, defeated the English at the Battle of Bannockburn, and Scotland remained unconquered by the English

Now a question arises, by which year did the English rule an area around the Dublin called the Pale?

At the beginning of the Middle Ages, Ireland was an independent country. The English first went to Ireland as troops to help the Irish king and decided to stay.

By 1200, the English ruled an area of Ireland known as the Pale, around Dublin. Some of the important lords in other parts of Ireland accepted the authority of the English king.

Zaina do you know which two wars were fought abroad during the Middle Ages?

No Idea Honey...

They Were:
1). Crusaders
2). Hundred Years War

Yes Zaina, listen carefully......
Many knights took part in the Crusades, in which European Christians fought for control of the Holy Land. English kings also fought a long war with France, called the Hundred Years War (even though it actually lasted 116 years).

Do you mean that the War lasted for 100 years?

One of the most famous battles of the Hundred Years War was the Battle of Agincourt in 1415, where King Henry V's vastly outnumbered English army defeated the French.
The English left France in the 1450s.

King Henry V's

Unbelievable, people used to fought for hundred years.
Oh my God...!!!

Zaina the next topic is "The Black Death"

"The Black Death"... Hmm...... Sounds scary.

The king gave land to his lords in return for help in war. Landowners had to send certain numbers of men to serve in the army. Some peasants had their own land but most were serfs.

59

Feudal Pyramid of Power

They had a small area of their lord's land where they could grow food. In return, they had to work for their lord and could not move away. The same system developed in southern Scotland.

In the north of Scotland and Ireland, land was owned by members of the 'clans' (prominent families).

Got it. Completely understand that. I will start taking Pratice tests on http://lifeintheuktest.biz

Now a question arises, what exactly is "The Black Death"?

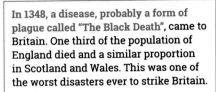

In 1348, a disease, probably a form of plague called "The Black Death", came to Britain. One third of the population of England died and a similar proportion in Scotland and Wales. This was one of the worst disasters ever to strike Britain.

Following the Black Death, the smaller population meant there was less need to grow cereal crops. There were labour shortages and peasants began to demand higher wages.

New social classes appeared, including owners of large areas of land called the gentry, and people left the countryside to live in the towns. In the towns, growing wealth led to the development of a strong middle class.

In Ireland, the Black Death killed many in the Pale and, for a time, the area controlled by the English became smaller.

Zaina now we are going to discuss about the Legal and political changes

Magna Carta

Okay, I am ready. Please go ahead.

In the Middle Ages, Parliament began to develop into the institution it is today. Its origins can be traced to the king's council of advisers, which included important noblemen and the leaders of the Church.

Magna Carta

The Magna is defined as a legal document signed by King John of England on June 15, 1215. **The Magna Carta** established the idea that even the king was subject to the law.

It protected the rights of the nobility and restricted the king's power to collect taxes or to make and change laws. In future, the king would need to involve his noblemen in decisions.

House of Lords:
The nobility, great landowners and bishops sat in House of Lords.

House of Commons:
Knights, who were usually smaller landowners, and wealthy people from towns and cities were elected to sit in the House of Commons.

A similar Parliament developed in Scotland. It had three Houses, called Estates: the lords, the commons and the clergy.

This was also a time of development in the legal system. The principle that judges are independent of the government began to be established. In England, judges developed 'common law' by a process of precedence (that is, following previous decisions) and tradition.

The British constitution is not written down in any single document, and therefore it is described as 'unwritten'.

In Scotland, the legal system developed slightly differently and laws were 'codified' (that is, written down).

It was a long topic Zaina, do you have any questions or confusion?

No, got it so far.

Great. But don't forget to take the practice tests on http://lifeintheuktest.biz

The Middle Ages saw the development of a national culture and identity. After the Norman Conquest, the king and his noblemen had spoken Norman French and the peasants had continued to speak Anglo-Saxon.

The king and his noblemen had spoken Norman French, for example, 'park' and 'beauty' – are based on Norman French words..

Peasants had continued to speak Anglo-Saxon, for example, 'apple', 'cow' and 'summer'.

Yes I know, gradually these two languages combined to become one language.

By 1400, in England, official documents were being written in English, and English had become the preferred language of the royal court and Parliament.

Geoffrey Chaucer

In the years leading up to 1400, Geoffrey Chaucer wrote a series of poems in English about a group of people going to Canterbury on a pilgrimage. The people decided to tell each other stories on the journey, and the poems describe the travellers and some of the stories they told. This collection of poems is called The Canterbury Tales.

Canterbury Tales

William Caxton

William Caxton Printing Press

The Canterbury Tales was one of the first books to be printed by William Caxton, the first person in England to print books using a printing press. Many of the stories are still popular. Some have been made into plays and television programmes.

In Scotland, many people continued to speak Gaelic and the Scots language also developed. A number of poets began to write in the Scots language.

John Barbour

Battle of Bannockburn

One example is John Barbour, who wrote The Bruce about the Battle of Bannockburn.

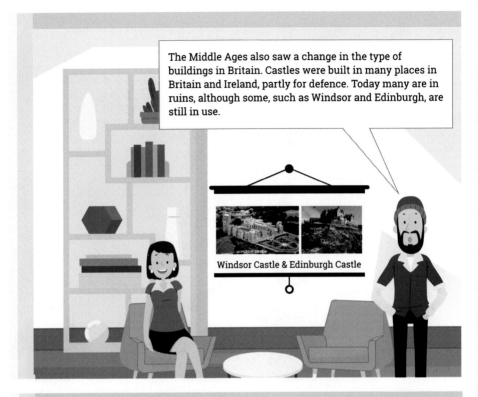

The Middle Ages also saw a change in the type of buildings in Britain. Castles were built in many places in Britain and Ireland, partly for defence. Today many are in ruins, although some, such as Windsor and Edinburgh, are still in use.

Windsor Castle & Edinburgh Castle

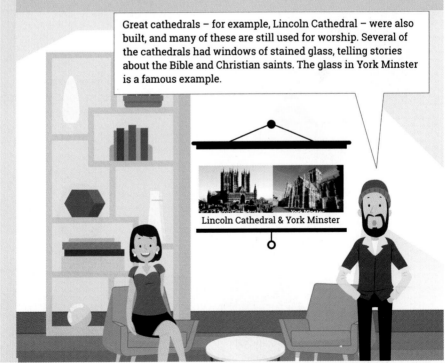

Great cathedrals – for example, Lincoln Cathedral – were also built, and many of these are still used for worship. Several of the cathedrals had windows of stained glass, telling stories about the Bible and Christian saints. The glass in York Minster is a famous example.

Lincoln Cathedral & York Minster

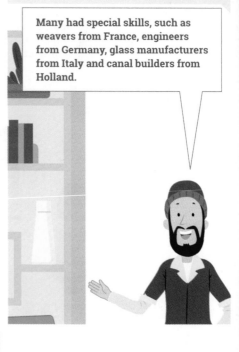

During this period, England was an important trading nation. English wool became a very important export. People came to England from abroad to trade and also to work.

Many had special skills, such as weavers from France, engineers from Germany, glass manufacturers from Italy and canal builders from Holland.

The glass in York Minster

Yes I have seen the The glass in York Minster. It really looks beautiful.

Now Zaina I'll tell you about the Wars of Roses, and how it got this name.
Please concentrate, it's a very important topic for the test.

Roses... Hmm sounds interesting. Please go ahead, I am listening.

Red Rose & White Rose

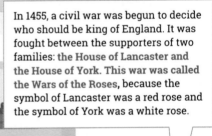

In 1455, a civil war was begun to decide who should be king of England. It was fought between the supporters of two families: the House of Lancaster and the House of York. This war was called the Wars of the Roses, because the symbol of Lancaster was a red rose and the symbol of York was a white rose.

Okay.
Please continue...

The war ended with the Battle of Bosworth Field in 1485. King Richard III of the House of York was killed in the battle and Henry Tudor, the leader of the House of Lancaster, became King Henry VII.

Henry then married King Richard's niece, Elizabeth of York, and united the two families. Henry was the first king of the House of Tudor.

Okay. So that's how they got married. Interesting history.

House Of Tudor

Henry was the first king of the House of Tudor. The symbol of the House of Tudor was a red rose with a white rose inside it as a sign that the Houses of York and Lancaster were now allies.

Zaina any questions so far? Or should we continue to our next topic "The Tudors and Stuarts"?

No. Let's continue...

Henry VII

After his victory in the Wars of the Roses, Henry VII wanted to make sure that England remained peaceful and that his position as king was secure. He deliberately strengthened the central administration of England and reduced the power of the nobles.

When he died, his son Henry VIII continued the policy of centralising power.
Henry VIII was most famous for breaking away from the Church of Rome and marrying six times.

Six times... Oh my God... Need to know in detail.

Yes Zaina, I am telling you. Please listen carefully.

Catherine

Anne Boleyn

His first wife was **Catherine of Aragon** – Catherine was a Spanish princess. She and Henry had a number of children but only one, Mary, survived. When Catherine wa too old to give him another child, Henry decided to divorce her, hoping that another wife would give him a son to be his heir.

His second wife was **Anne Boleyn** – Anne Boleyn was English. She and Henry had one daughter, Elizabeth. Anne was unpopular in the country and was accused of taking lovers. She was executed at the tower of London.

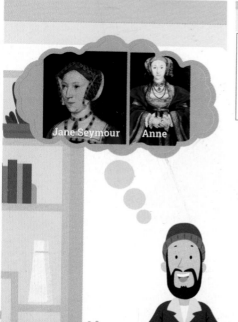

His third wife was **Jane Seymour** – Henry married Jane after Anne's execution. She gave Henry the son he wanted, Edward, but she died shortly after his birth.

His fourth wife was **Anne of Cleves** – Anne was a German princess. Henry married her for political reasons but divorced her soon after.

His fifth wife was **Catherine Howard** – Catherine was a cousin of Anne Boleyn. She was also accused of taking lovers and executed.

His sixth wife was **Catherine Parr** – Catherine was a widow who married Henry later in his life. She survived him and married again but died soon after.

I am stunned....

To divorce his first wife, Henry needed the approval of the Pope. When the Pope refused, Henry established the church of England. In this new church, the king, not the Pope, would have the power to appoint bishops and order how people should worship.

The Protestants formed their own churches. They read the Bible in their own languages instead of Latin; they did not pray to saints or at shrines; and they believed that a person's own relationship with God was more important than submitting to the authority of the Church.

During the 16th century, Protestants gained strength in England, Wales and Scotland.

At the same time the Reformation was happening across Europe. This was a movement against the authority of the Pope and the ideas and practices of the Roman Catholic Church.

During the reign of Henry VIII, Wales became formally united with England by the Act for the Government of Wales. The Welsh sent representatives to the House of Commons and the Welsh legal system was reformed.

Edward VI

Henry VIII was succeeded by his son Edward VI, who was strongly Protestant. During his reign, the Book of Common Prayer was written to be used in the Church of England. A version of this book is still used in some churches today. Edward died at the age of 15 after ruling for just over six years, and his half-sister Mary became queen.

Mary was a devout Catholic and persecuted Protestants (for this reason, she became known as 'Bloody Mary'). Mary also died after a short reign and the next monarch was her half-sister, Elizabeth, the daughter of Henry VIII and Anne Boleyn.

Oh my God... 'Bloody Mary', very scary name.

Yes. Now we will move on to Queen Elizabeth I, she was a Protestant. She re-established the Church of England as the official Church of England.

Queen Elizabeth I

Everyone had to attend their local church and there were laws about the type of religious services and the prayers which could be said, but Elizabeth did not ask about people's real beliefs.

Oh Wow...
That means she was successful in avoiding serious religious conflict within England.

She succeeded in finding a balance between the views of the Catholics and the more extreme Protestants.

Spanish Armada

Elizabeth became one of the most popular monarchs in English history, particularly after 1588, when the English defeated the Spanish Armada (a large fleet of ships), which had been sent by Spain to conquer England and restore Catholicism.

Mary, Queen of Scots

Now I'll explain about The Reformation in Scotland and Mary, Queen of Scots

Okay...

Scotland had also been strongly influenced by Protestant ideas. In 1560, the predominantly Protestant Scottish Parliament abolished the authority of the Pope in Scotland and Roman Catholic religious services became illegal.

Protestant Church of Scotland with an elected leadership was established but, unlike in England, this was not a state Church.

The queen of Scotland, Mary Stuart (often now called 'Mary, Queen of Scots') was a Catholic. She was only a week old when her father died and she became queen.

Much of her childhood was spent in France. When she returned to Scotland, she was the centre of a power struggle between different groups. When her husband was murdered, Mary was suspected of involvement and fled to England. She gave her throne to her Protestant son, James VI of Scotland.

Oh My....

Mary Stuart Execution

Mary was Elizabeth I's cousin and hoped that Elizabeth might help her, but Elizabeth suspected Mary of wanting to take over the English throne, and kept her prisoner for 20 years. Mary was eventually executed, accused of plotting against Elizabeth I.

Elizabethan Period

The Elizabethan period in England was a time of growing patriotism: a feeling of pride in being English, English explorers sought new trade routes and tried to expand British trade into the Spanish colonies in the Americas.

Sir Francis Drake

Sir Francis Drake, one of the commanders in the defeat of the Spanish Armada, was one of the founders of England's naval tradition.

Golden Hind

His ship, the Golden Hind, was one of the first to sail right around ('circumnavigate') the world.

Colonisation

In Elizabeth I's time, English settlers first began to colonise the eastern coast of America. This colonisation, particularly by people who disagreed with the religious views of the next two kings, greatly increased in the next century.

The Elizabethan period is also remembered for the richness of its poetry and drama, especially the plays and poems of William Shakespeare.

Ahaa! Everybody knows about him. He was a playwright and actor and wrote many poems and plays.

William Shakespeare

William Shakespeare (1564-1616) was born in Stratford-upon-Avon, England.
As 18 years old married Anne Hathaway. His plays were on London Stage by 1592. From 1594 his plays performed only Lord Chamberlain's Men.

Ahaa... OK.

Zaina do you know the names of his most famous plays?

Yes, I know, his most famous plays include A Midsummer Night's dream, Hamlet, Macbeth and Romeo and Juliet.

Right Zaina...
He also dramatised significant events from the past, but he did not focus solely on kings and queens. He was one of the first to portray ordinary Englishmen and women.

Shakespeare had a great influence on the English language and invented many words that are still common today.

Lines from his plays and poems which are often still quoted include:
- Once more unto the breach (Henry V)
- To be or not to be (Hamlet)
- A rose by any other name (Romeo and Juliet)
- All the world's a stage (As You Like It)
- The darling buds of May (Sonnet 18 – Shall I Compare Thee To A Summer's Day)

Hmm.... OK.

Many people regard Shakespeare as the greatest playwright of all time. His plays and poems are still performed and studied in Britain and other countries today. The Globe Theatre in London is a modern copy of the theatres in which his plays were first performed.

James VI

Elizabeth I never married and so had no children of her own to inherit her throne. When she died in 1603 her heir was her cousin James VI of Scotland.

He became King James I of England, Wales and Ireland but Scotland remained a separate country.

Oh Wow...

James VI

One achievement of King James' reign was a new translation of the Bible into English. This translation is known as the 'King James Version' or the 'Authorised Version'.

KING JAMES BIBLE

It was not the first English Bible but is a version which continues to be used in many Protestant churches today.

James VI

During the reigns of Elizabeth I and James I, many people in Ireland opposed rule by the Protestant government in England. There were a number of rebellions.

The English government encouraged Scottish and English Protestants to settle in Ulster, the northern province of Ireland, taking over the land from Catholic landholders.

Hmm.... OK...

These settlements were known as plantations. Many of the new settlers came from south-west Scotland and other land was given to companies based in London.

James later organised similar plantations in several other parts of Ireland. This had serious longterm consequence for the history of England, Scotland and Ireland.

Hmm.... Got it...

James I and his son Charles I were less skilled politically. Both believed in the 'Divine Right of Kings': the idea that the king was directly appointed by God to rule. They thought that the king should be able to act without having to seek approval from Parliament.

Charles I

When Charles I inherited the thrones of England, Wales, Ireland and Scotland, he tried to rule in line with this principle. When he could not get Parliament to agree with his religious and foreign policies, he tried to rule without the Parliament at all.

For 11 years, he found ways in which to raise money without Parliament's approval but eventually trouble in Scotland meant that he had to recall Parliament.

Interesting....

Charles I

Charles I wanted the worship of the Church of England to include more ceremony and introduced a revise Prayer Book. He tried to impose this Prayer Book on the Presbyterian Church in Scotland and this led to serious unrest.

A Scottish army was formed and Charles could not find the money he needed for his own army without the help of Parliament. In 1640, he recalled Parliament to ask it for funds. Many in Parliament were Puritans, a group of Protestants who advocated strict and simple religious doctrine and worship. They did not agree with the king's religious views and disliked his reforms of the Church of England. Parliament refused to give the king the money he asked for, even after the Scottish army invaded England.

Another rebellion began in Ireland because the Roman Catholics in Ireland were afraid of the growing power of the Puritans. Parliament took this opportunity to demand control of the English army – a change that would have transferred substantial power from the king to Parliament.

In response, Charles I entered the House of Commons and tried to arrest five parliamentary leaders, but they had been warned and were not there. (No monarch has set foot in the Commons since.)

Civil war between the king and Parliament could not now be avoided and began in 1642. The country spilt into those who supported the king (the Cavaliers) and those who supported Parliament (the Roundheads).

Oliver Cromwell

The king's army was defeated at the Battles of Marston Moor and Naseby. By 1646, it was clear that the Parliament had won the war.

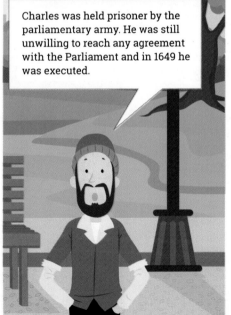

Charles was held prisoner by the parliamentary army. He was still unwilling to reach any agreement with the Parliament and in 1649 he was executed.

England declared itself a republic, called the Commonwealth. It no longer had a monarch. For a time, it was not totally clear how the country would be governed.

For now, the army was in control. One of its generals, Oliver Cromwell, was sent to Ireland, where the revolt which had begun in 1641 still continued and where there was still a Royalist army.

Cromwell was successful in establishing the authority of the English Parliament but did this with such violence that even today Cromwell remains a controversial figure in Ireland.

Ahaa...

Charles II

The Scots had not agreed to the execution of Charles I and declared his son Charles II to be king. He was crowned king of Scotland and led a Scottish army into England. Cromwell defeated this army in the Battles of Dunbar and Worcester.

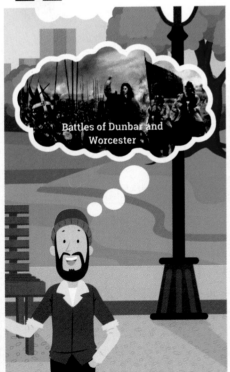

Battles of Dunbar and Worcester

Charles II escaped from Worcester, famously hiding in an oak tree on one occasion, and eventually fled to Europe. Parliament now controlled Scotland as well as England and Wales.

After his campaign in Ireland and victory over Charles II at Worcester, Cromwell was recognised as the leader of the new republic. **He was given the title of Lord Protector and ruled until his death in 1658.**

When Cromwell died, his son, Richard, became Lord Protector in his place but was not able to control the army or the government. Although Britain had been a republic for 11 years, without Oliver Cromwell there was no clear leader or system of government.

Many people in the country wanted stability. People began to talk about the need for a king. The Restoration, in May 1660, Parliament invited Charles II to come back from exile in The Netherlands. He was crowned King Charles II of England, Wales, Scotland and Ireland.

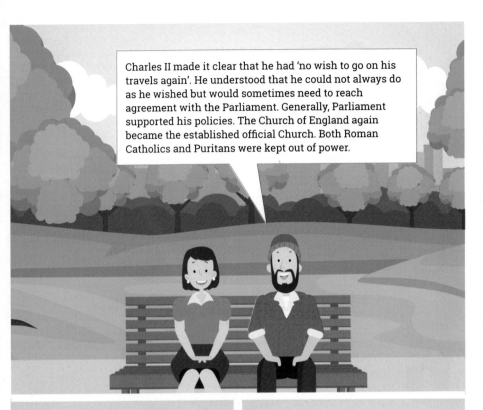

Charles II made it clear that he had 'no wish to go on his travels again'. He understood that he could not always do as he wished but would sometimes need to reach agreement with the Parliament. Generally, Parliament supported his policies. The Church of England again became the established official Church. Both Roman Catholics and Puritans were kept out of power.

Plague in London

During Charles II's reign, in 1665, there was a major outbreak of plague in London. Thousands of people died, especially in poorer areas.

The following year, a great fire destroyed much of the city, including many churches and St Paul's Cathedral. London was rebuilt with a new St Paul's, which was designed by a famous architect, Sir Christopher Wren.

Samuel Pepys wrote about these events in a diary which was later published and is still read today.

Habeas Corpus Act

The Habeas Corpus Act became law in 1679. This was a very important piece of legislation which remains relevant today. Habeas corpus is Latin for 'you must present the person in court'. The Act guaranteed that no one could be held prisoner unlawfully. Every prisoner has a right to a court hearing.

Isaac Newton

Charles II was interested in science. During his reign, the Royal Society was formed to promote 'natural knowledge'. This is the oldest surviving scientific society in the world. Among its early members were Sir Edmund Halley who successfully predicted the return of the comet now called Halley's Comet, and Sir Isaac Newton.

Born in Lincolnshire, eastern England, Isaac Newton first became interested in science when he studied at Cambridge University. He became an important figure in the field.

His most famous published work was Philosophiae Naturalis Principia Mathematica ('Mathematical Principle of Natural Philosophy'), which showed how gravity applied to the whole universe. Newton also discovered that white light is made up of the colours of the rainbow. Many of his discoveries are still important for modern science.

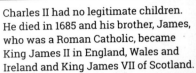

Charles II had no legitimate children. He died in 1685 and his brother, James, who was a Roman Catholic, became King James II in England, Wales and Ireland and King James VII of Scotland.

James II's elder daughter, Mary, was married to her cousin William of Orange, the Protestant ruler of the Netherlands. In 1688, important Protestants in England asked William to invade England and proclaim himself king. When William reached England, there was no resistance.

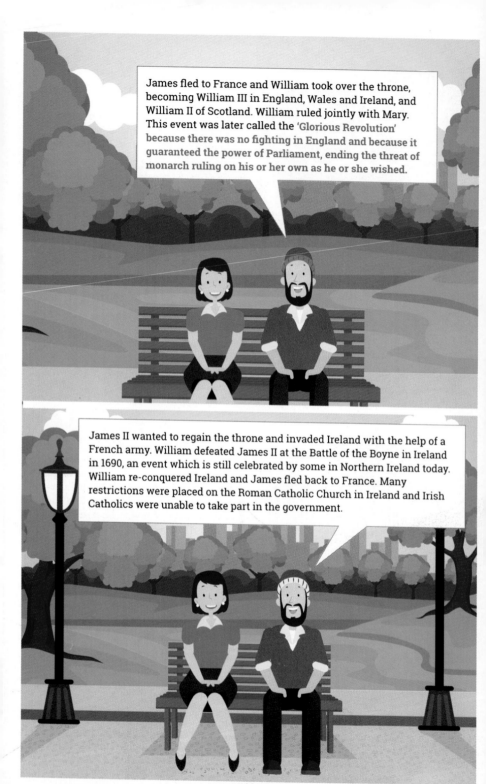

James fled to France and William took over the throne, becoming William III in England, Wales and Ireland, and William II of Scotland. William ruled jointly with Mary. This event was later called the 'Glorious Revolution' because there was no fighting in England and because it guaranteed the power of Parliament, ending the threat of monarch ruling on his or her own as he or she wished.

James II wanted to regain the throne and invaded Ireland with the help of a French army. William defeated James II at the Battle of the Boyne in Ireland in 1690, an event which is still celebrated by some in Northern Ireland today. William re-conquered Ireland and James fled back to France. Many restrictions were placed on the Roman Catholic Church in Ireland and Irish Catholics were unable to take part in the government.

There was also support for James in Scotland. An attempt at an armed rebellion in support of James was quickly defeated at Killiecrankie. All Scottish clans were required formally to accept William as king by taking an oath.

The MacDonalds of Glencoe were late in taking an oath. The memory of this massacre meant some Scots distrusted the new government.

Some continued to believe that James was the rightful king, particularly in Scotland. Some joined him in exile in France; others were secret supporters. James' supporters became known as Jacobites.

The Bill of Rights, 1689, confirmed the rights of Parliament and the limits of the king's power. This confirmed that the king would no longer be able to raise taxes and administer justice without agreement from Parliament.

The balance of power between monarch and Parliament had now permanently changed. The Bill of Rights, 1689, confirmed the rights of Parliament and the limits of the king's power. Parliament took control of who could be monarch and declared that the king or queen must be a Protestant.

A new Parliament had to be elected at least every three years (later this became seven years and now it is five years). Every year the monarch had to ask Parliament to renew funding for the army and the navy.

This was also an important time for the development of a free press (newspapers and other publications which are not controlled by the government). From 1695, newspapers were allowed to operate without a government licence. Increasing numbers of newspapers began to be published.

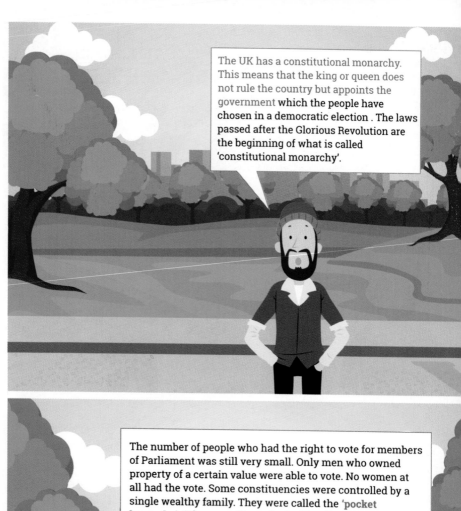

The UK has a constitutional monarchy. This means that the king or queen does not rule the country but appoints the government which the people have chosen in a democratic election . The laws passed after the Glorious Revolution are the beginning of what is called 'constitutional monarchy'.

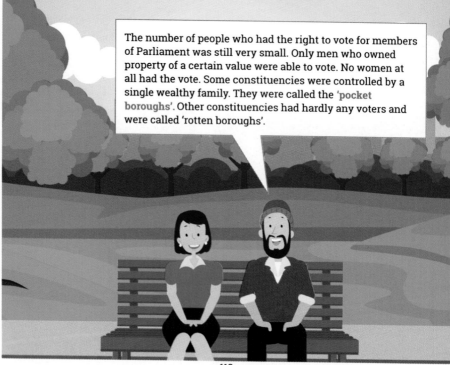

The number of people who had the right to vote for members of Parliament was still very small. Only men who owned property of a certain value were able to vote. No women at all had the vote. Some constituencies were controlled by a single wealthy family. They were called the 'pocket boroughs'. Other constituencies had hardly any voters and were called 'rotten boroughs'.

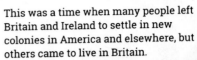This was a time when many people left Britain and Ireland to settle in new colonies in America and elsewhere, but others came to live in Britain.

The first Jews to come to Britain since the Middle Ages settled in London in 1656.

Refugees from France

Between 1680 and 1720 many refugees called **Huguenots** came from France. They were Protestants and had been persecuted for their religion. Many were educated and skilled and worked as scientists, in banking, or in weaving or other crafts.

William and Mary's successor, Queen Anne, had no surviving children. This created uncertainty over the succession in England, Wales and Ireland and in Scotland. The Act of Union, known as the Treaty of Union in Scotland, was therefore agreed in 1707, creating the Kingdom of Great Britain. Although Scotland was no longer an independent country, it kept its own legal and education systems and Presbyterian Church.

George I

When Queen Anne died in 1714, Parliament chose a German, George I, to be the next king, because he was Anne's nearest Protestant relative. An attempt by Scottish Jacobites to put James II's son on the throne instead was quickly defeated.

Sir Robert Walpole First Prime Minister

George I did not speak very good English and this increased his need to rely on his ministers. The most important minister in Parliament became known as the Prime Minister. The first man to be called this was Sir Robert Walpole, who was Prime Minister from 1721 to 1742.

Charles Edward Stuart

In 1745 there was another attempt to put a Stuart king back on the throne in place of George I's son, George II. Charles Edward Stuart (Bonnie Prince Charlie), the grandson of James II, landed in Scotland.

Battle of Culloden in 1746

He was supported by clansmen from the Scottish highlands and raised an army. Charles initially had some successes but was defeated by George II's army at the Battle of Culloden in 1746. Charles escaped back to Europe.

'Highland Clearances'.

A process began which became known as the 'Highland Clearances'. Many Scottish landlords destroyed individual small farms (known as 'crofts') to make space for large flocks of sheep and cattle. Evictions became very common in the early 19th century. Many Scottish people left for North America at this time.

Known in Scotland as 'The Bard', Robert Burns was a Scottish poet. He wrote in the Scots language, English with some Scottish words and standard English. He also revised a lot of the traditional folk songs by changing or adding lyrics. Burns' best-known work is probably the song Auld Lang Syne, which is sung by people in the UK and other countries when they are celebrating the New Year (or Hogmanay as it is called in Scotland).

Robert Burns

Adam Smith

During the 18th century, new ideas about politics, philosophy and science were developed. This is often called 'the Enlightenment'. Many of the great thinkers of the Enlightenment were Scottish. Adam Smith developed ideas about economics which are still referred to today.

Oh.... Wow...

The Industrial Revolution was the rapid development of industry in Britain in the 18th and 19th centuries. Britain was the first country to industrialise on a large scale. It happened because of the development of machinery and the use of steam power.

Agriculture and the manufacturing of goods became mechanised. This made things more efficient and increased production. Coal and other raw materials were needed to power the new factories. Many people moved from the countryside and started working in the mining and manufacturing industries.

Bessemer Process

The development of the Bessemer process for the mass production of steel led to the development of the ship building industry and the railways. Manufacturing jobs became the main source of employment in Britain.

Born in 1732, Arkwright originally trained and worked as a barber. He was able to dye hair and make wigs. When wigs became less popular, he started to work in textiles. He improved the original carding machine. Arkwright is particularly remembered for the efficient and profitable way that he ran his factories.

Richard Arkwright

Working conditions during the Industrial Revolution were very poor. There were no laws to protect employees, who were often forced to work long hours in dangerous situations. Children also worked and were treated in the same way as adults.

Captain James Cook

This was also a time of increased colonisation overseas. Captain James Cook mapped the coast of Australia and a few colonies were established there. Britain gained control over Canada, and the East India Company, originally set up to trade, gained control of large parts of India.

Britain traded all over the world and began to import more goods. Sugar and tobacco came from North America and the west Indies; textiles, tea and spices came from India and the area that is today called Indonesia.

Some continued to believe that James was the rightful king, particularly in Scotland. Some joined him in exile in France; others were secret supporters. James' supporters became known as Jacobites.

In 1810 he opened the Hindoostane Coffee House in George Street, London. It was the first curry house to open in Britain. Mahomet and his wife also introduced 'shampooing', the Indian art of head massage, to Britain.

Sake Dean Mahomat

Lovely Curry, I love Indian Foods.

The first formal anti-slavery groups were set up by the Quakers in the late 1700s, and they petitioned Parliament to ban the practice. William Wilberforce, an evangelical Christian and a member of Parliament, also played an important part in changing the law. Along with other abolitionists (people who supported the abolition of slavery), he succeeded in turning public opinion against the slave trade.

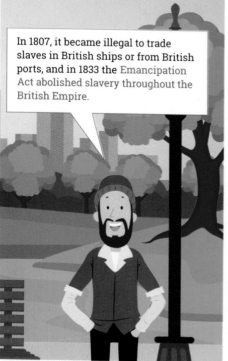

In 1807, it became illegal to trade slaves in British ships or from British ports, and in 1833 the Emancipation Act abolished slavery throughout the British Empire.

Wow... Good Good...

The Royal Navy stopped slave ships from other countries, freed the slaves and punished the slave traders. After 1833, 2 million Indian and Chinese workers were employed to replace the freed slaves.

In 1776, 13 American colonies declared their independence, stating that people had a right to establish their own governments. The colonists eventually defeated the British army and Britain recognised the colonies' independence in 1783.

By the 1760s, there were substantial British colonies in North America. The colonies were wealthy and largely in control of their own affairs. Many of the colonist families had originally gone to North America in order to have religious freedom. They were well educated and interested in ideas of liberty. The British government wanted to tax the colonies.

During the 18th century, Britain fought a number of wars with France. In 1789, there was a revolution in France and the new French government soon declared war on Britain. Napoleon, who became Emperor of France, continued the war.

Admiral Nelson

Admiral Nelson

Britain's navy fought against combined French and Spanish fleets, winning the Battle of Trafalgar in 1805. Admiral Nelson was in charge of the British fleet at Trafalgar and was killed in the battle. Nelson's Column (Pillar) in Trafalgar Square, London, is a monument to him. His ship, HMS Victory, can be visited in Portsmouth.

Napoleon

Duke Of Wellington

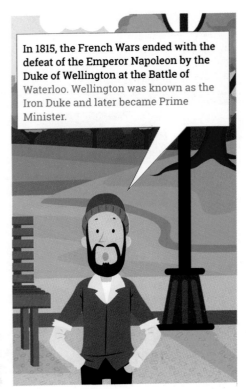

In 1815, the French Wars ended with the defeat of the Emperor Napoleon by the Duke of Wellington at the Battle of Waterloo. Wellington was known as the Iron Duke and later became Prime Minister.

St. George's Cross of England

+

St. Andrew's Cross of Scotland

Union Flag of the UK

+

St. Patrick's Cross of Ireland

The crosses of the three countries which combined to form the Union Flag

One symbol of this union between England, Scotland, Wales and Ireland was a new version of the official flag, the Union Flag. This is often called the Union Jack.

In 1606

In 1801

There is also an official Welsh flag, which shows a Welsh dragon. The Welsh dragon does not appear on the Union Flag because, when the first Union Flag was created in 1606 from the flags of Scotland and England, the Principality of Wales was already untied with England.

Queen Victoria

In 1837, Queen Victoria became queen of the UK at the age of 18. She reigned until 1901, almost 64 years. At the date of writing (2013) this is the longest reign of any British monarch. Her reign is known as the Victorian Age.

During the Victorian period, the British Empire grew to cover all of India, Australia and large parts of Africa. It became the largest empire the world has ever seen, with an estimated population of more than 400 million people.

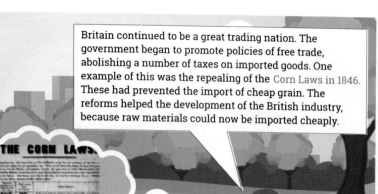

Britain continued to be a great trading nation. The government began to promote policies of free trade, abolishing a number of taxes on imported goods. One example of this was the repealing of the Corn Laws in 1846. These had prevented the import of cheap grain. The reforms helped the development of the British industry, because raw materials could now be imported cheaply.

Working conditions in factories gradually became better. In 1847, the number of hours that women and children could work was limited by law to 10 hours per day. Better housing began to be built for workers.

Transport links also improved, enabling goods and people to move more easily around the country. Just before Victoria came to the throne, the father and son George and Robert Stephenson pioneered the "Railway Engine".

George and Robert Stephenson

Railway Engine

and a major expansion of the railways took place in the Victorian period. Railways were built throughout the Empire. There were also great advances in other areas, such as the building of bridges by engineers such as Isambard Kingdom Brunel.

Clifton Suspension Bridge

Isambard Kingdom Brunel

Brunel was originally from Portsmouth, England. He was an engineer who built tunnels, bridges, railway lines and ships. He was responsible for constructing the Great Western Railway and the Clifton Suspension Bridge.

British industry led the world in the 19th century. The UK produced more than half of the world's iron, coal and cotton cloth. The UK also became a centre for financial services, including insurance and banking.

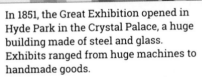

In 1851, the Great Exhibition opened in Hyde Park in the Crystal Palace, a huge building made of steel and glass. Exhibits ranged from huge machines to handmade goods.

Countries from all over the world showed their goods but most of the objects were made in Britain.

- French Empire
- Ottoman Empire
- Great Britain
- Kingdom of Sardinia

vs. Russia

Crimea

Russia's attempts to occupy
Crimea led to the Crimean War.

From 1853 to 1856, Britain fought with Turkey and France against Russia in the Crimean War. It was the first war to be extensively covered by the media through news stories and photographs. The conditions were very poor and many soldiers died from illnesses they caught in the hospitals, rather than from war wounds. Queen Victoria introduced the Victoria Cross medal during this war.

In 1860 she established the Nightingale Training School for nurses at St Thomas' Hospital in London. The school was the first of its kind and still exists today, as do many of the practices that Florence used. She is often regarded as the founder of modern nursing.

Florence Nightingale

A million people died from disease and starvation. Another million and a half left Ireland. Some emigrated to the United States and others came to England. By 1861 there were large populations of Irish people in cities such as Liverpool, London, Manchester and Glasgow.

In 1830's and 1840's, a group called the Chartists campaigned for reform. They wanted six changes:
- for every man to have the vote
- elections every year
- for all regions to be equal in the electoral system
- secret ballots
- for any man to be able to stand as an MP
- for Mp's to be paid

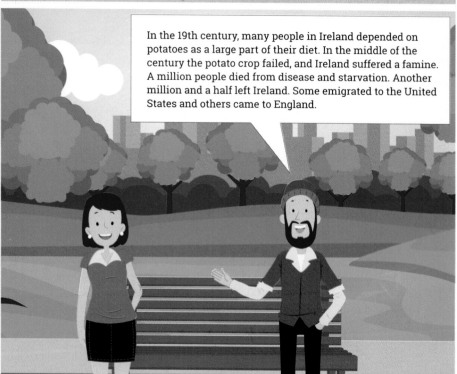

In the 19th century, many people in Ireland depended on potatoes as a large part of their diet. In the middle of the century the potato crop failed, and Ireland suffered a famine. A million people died from disease and starvation. Another million and a half left Ireland. Some emigrated to the United States and others came to England.

Suffragettes

In the late 19th and early 20th centuries, an increasing number of women campaigned and demonstrated for greater rights and, in particular, the right to vote. They formed the women's suffrage movement and became known as the 'suffragettes'.

Emmeline Pankhurst was born in Manchester in 1858. She set up the women's Franchise League in 1889, which fought to get the vote in local elections for married women. In 1903 she helped found the Women's Social and Political Union (WSPU).

VOTES FOR WOMEN
Emmeline Pankhurst

This was the first group whose members were called 'suffragettes', which fought to get the vote in local elections for married women. In 1918, women over the age of 30 were given voting rights. Shortly before Emmeline's death in 1928, women were given the right to vote at the age of 21, the same as men.

Boer War of 1899

The Boer War of 1899 to 1902 made the discussions about the future of the Empire more urgent. The British went to war in South Africa with settlers from the Netherlands called the Boers. The Boers fought fiercely and the war went on for over three years.

Many died in the fighting and many more from disease. There was some public sympathy for the Boers and people began to question whether the Empire could continue.

By the second half of the 20th century, there was, for the most part, an orderly transition from Empire to Commonwealth, with countries being granted their independence.

Rudyard Kipling was born in India in 1865 and later lived in India, the UK and the USA. He wrote books and poems set in both India and the UK. His poems and novels reflected the idea that the British Empire was a force for good. Kipling was awarded the Nobel Prize in Literature in 1907.

Rudyard Kipling

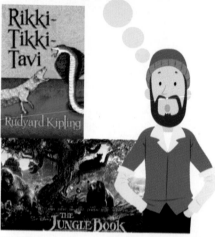

His books include the Just So Stories and The Jungle Book, which continue to be popular today. His poem If has often been voted among the UK's favourite poems.

Working conditions in factories gradually became better. In 1847, the number of hours that women and children could work was limited by law to 10 hours per day. Better housing began to be built for workers.

Transport links also improved, enabling goods and people to move more easily around the country. Just before Victoria came to the throne, the father and son George and Robert Stephenson pioneered the "Railway Engine".

The early 20th century was a time of optimism in Britain. The nation, with its expansive Empire, well-admired navy, thriving industry and strong political institutions, was what is now known as a global 'superpower'.

Financial help for the unemployed, old-age pensions and free school meals were just a few of the important measures introduced.

Assassination of Archduke Franz Ferdinand

The assassination of Archduke Franz Ferdinand in Sarajevo on On 28 June 1914, it triggered a chain of events that resulted in World War 1. The Allies fought against the Central Powers – mainly Germany, the Austro-Hungarian Empire, the Ottoman Empire and later Bulgaria.

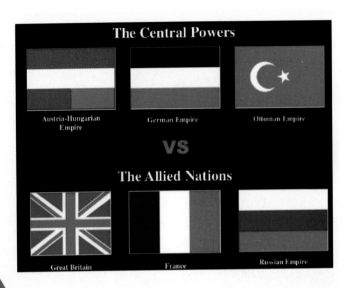

The Central Powers

Austria-Hungarian Empire · German Empire · Ottoman Empire

VS

The Allied Nations

Great Britain · France · Russian Empire

Britain, France, Ireland and Russia were part of an alliance called the Triple Entente, while Germany aligned itself with Austria-Hungary - known as Central Powers.

The whole of the British Empire was involved in the conflict – for example, more than a million Indians fought on behalf of Britain in lots of different countries, and around 40, 000 were killed.

World War I

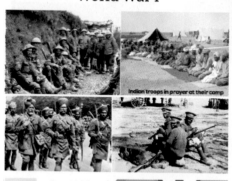

Indian troops in prayer at their camp

Men from the West Indies, Africa, Australia, New Zealand and Canada also fought with the British. The Allies fought against the Central Powers – mainly Germany, the Austro-Hungarian Empire, the Ottoman Empire and later Bulgaria.

Millions of people were killed or wounded, with more than 2 million British casualties. One battle, the British attack of the Somme in July 1916, resulted in about 60,000 British casualties on the first day alone.

The First World War ended at 11.00 am on 11th November 1918 with victory for Britain and its allies.

Remembrance Day, 11 November, commemorates those who died fighting for the UK and its allies. Originally it commemorated the dead of the First World War, which ended on 11 November 1918. People wear poppies (the red flower found on the battlefields of the First World War). **At 11.00 am there is a two-minute silence** and wreaths are laid at the Cenotaph in Whitehall, London.

Remembrance Day

In 1913, the British government promised 'Home Rule' for Ireland. The proposal was to have a self-governing Ireland with its own parliament but still part of the UK.

A Home Rule Bill was introduced in Parliament. It was opposed by the Protestants in the north of Ireland, who threatened to resist Home Rule by force.

The outbreak of the First World War led the British government to postpone any changes in Ireland. Irish Nationalists were not willing to wait and in 1916 there was an uprising (the Easter Rising) against the British in Dublin. The leaders of the uprising were executed under military law. A guerrilla war against the British army and the police in Ireland followed. In 1921 a peace treaty was signed and in 1922 Ireland became two countries.

The conflict between those wishing for full Irish independence and those wishing to remain loyal to the British government is often referred to as 'the Troubles'.

In the 1920s, many people's living conditions got better. There were improvements in public housing and new homes were built in many towns and cities.

However, in 1929, the world entered the 'Great Depression' and some parts of the UK suffered mass unemployment. The effects of the depression of the 1930s were felt differently in different parts of the UK.

The traditional heavy industries such as shipbuilding were badly affected but new industries – including the automobile and aviation industries – developed.

"We can only see a short distance ahead, but we can see plenty there that needs to be done."

– Alan Turing
the father of modern computer science

A Turing machine is a theoretical mathematical device invented by Alan Turing (1912-54), a British mathematician, in the 1930s. The theory was influential in the development of computer science and the modern-day computer.

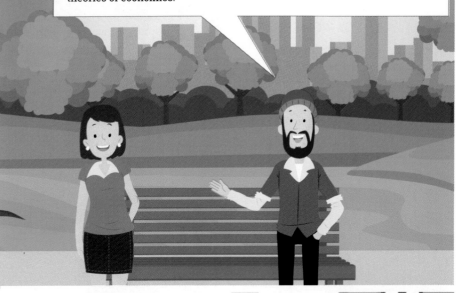

Car ownership doubled from 1 million to 2 million between 1930 and 1939. In addition, many new houses were built. It was also a time of cultural blossoming, with writers such as Graham Greene and Evelyn Waugh prominent. The economist John Maynard Keynes published influential new theories of economics.

Evelyn Waugh

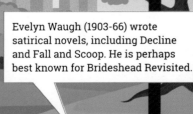

Evelyn Waugh (1903-66) wrote satirical novels, including Decline and Fall and Scoop. He is perhaps best known for Brideshead Revisited.

Scotsman John Logie Baird

Oh WOW....

The television was developed by Scotsman John Logie Baird (1888-1946) in the 1920s. In 1932 he made the first television broadcast between London and Glasgow.

150

Adolf Hitler came to power in Germany in 1933. He believed that the conditions imposed on Germany by the Allies after the First World War were unfair; he also wanted to conquer more land for the German people. He set about renegotiating treaties, building up arms, and testing Germany's military strength in nearby countries.

The British government tried to avoid another war. However, when Hitler invaded Poland in 1939, Britain and France declared war in order to stop his aggression.

That was First World War, now please tell me about the Second World War.

Yes Zaina, please listen carefully...

The war was initially fought between the Axis powers (fascist Germany and Italy and the Empire of Japan) and the Allies. The main countries on the allied side were the UK, France, Poland, Australia, New Zealand, Canada, and the Union of South Africa.

The most important planes used by the Royal Air Force in the Battle of Britain were the Spitfire and the Hurricane – which were designed and built in Britain.

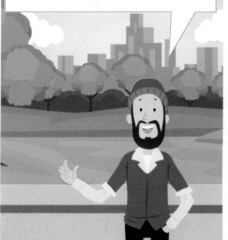

Despite winning the Battle of Britain, the German air force was able to continue bombing London and other British cities at night-time. **This was called the Blitz.**

Many civilian volunteers in small pleasure and fishing boats from Britain helped the Navy to rescue more than 300,000 men from the beaches around Dunkirk. Although many lives and a lot of equipment were lost, the evacuation was a success and meant that Britain was better able to continue the fight against the Germans. The evacuation gave rise to the phrase 'the Dunkirk spirit'.

Winston Churchill

Now some facts about Sir Winston Churchill

Churchill was the son of a politician and, before becoming a Conservative MP in 1900, was a soldier and journalist. In May 1940 he became Prime Minister. He refused to surrender to the Nazis and was an inspirational leader to the British people in a time of hardship. He lost the General Election in 1945 but returned as Prime Minister in 1951.

He was an MP until he stood down at the 1964 General Election. Following his death in 1965, he was given a state funeral.

He remains a much admired figure to this day, and in 2002 was voted the greatest Briton of all time by the public.

During the War, he made many famous speeches including lines which you may still hear:
'I have nothing to offer but blood, toil, tears and sweat'
Churchill's first speech to the House of Commons after he became Prime Minister, 1940.

'We shall fight on the beaches,
we shall fight on the landing grounds,
we shall fight in the fields and in the streets,
we shall fight in the hills;
we shall never surrender' speech to the House of Commons after Dunkirk, 1940

On 6 June 1944, allied forces landed in Normandy (this event is often referred to as 'D-Day'). Following victory on the beaches of Normandy, the allied forces pressed on through France and eventually into Germany. The Allies comprehensively defeated Germany in May 1945.

Ernest Rutherford

Scientists led by Ernest Rutherford, working at Manchester and then Cambridge University, were the first to 'split the atom' and took part in the Manhattan Project in the United States, which developed the atomic bomb.

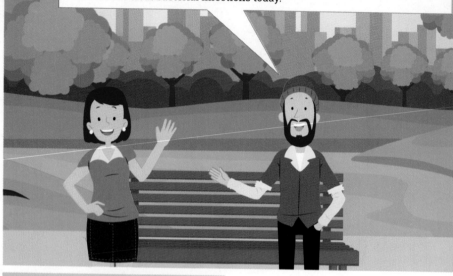

Born in Scotland, Fleming moved to London as a teenager and later qualified as a doctor. He was researching influenza (the 'flu') in 1928 when he discovered penicillin. This was then further developed into a usable drug by the scientists Howard Florey and Ernst Chain. By the 1940s it was in mass production. Fleming won the Nobel Prize in Medicine in 1945. Penicillin is still used to treat bacterial infections today.

Alexander Fleming

Zaina let's head back home.

Alexander Fleming

Although the UK had won the war, the country was exhausted economically and the people wanted change. During the war, there had been significant reforms to the educational system and people now looked for wider social reforms.

Clement Attlee

In 1945 the British people elected a Labour government. The new Prime Minister was Clement Attlee, who promised to introduce the welfare state outlined in the Beveridge Report.

In 1948, Aneurin (Nye) Bevan, the Minister for Health, led the establishment of the National Health Service (NHS), which guaranteed a minimum standard of health care for all, free at the point of use.

Aneurin (Nye) Bevan

A national system of benefits was also introduced to provide 'social security', so that the population would be protected from the 'cradle to the grave'.

The government took into public ownership (nationalised) the railways, coal mines and gas, water and electricity supplies.

In 1947, independence was granted to nine countries, including India, Pakistan and Ceylon (now Sri Lanka). Other colonies in Africa, the Caribbean and the Pacific achieved independence over the next 20 years.

The UK developed its own atomic bomb and joined the new North Atlantic Treaty Organization (NATO), an alliance of nations set up to resist the perceived threat of invasion by the Soviet Union and it allies.

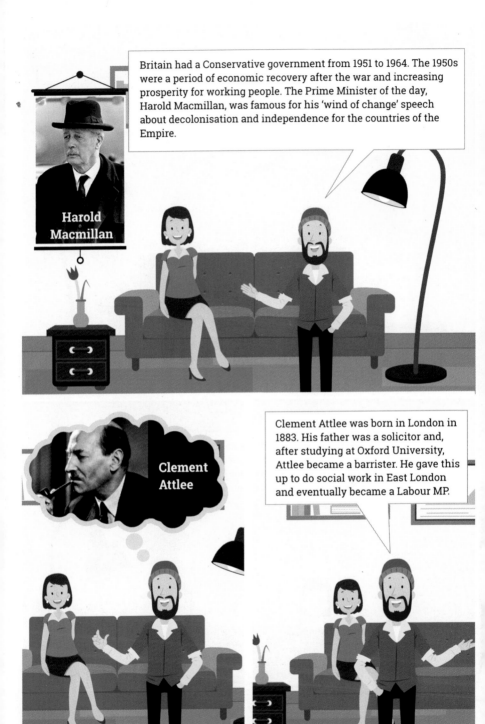

Britain had a Conservative government from 1951 to 1964. The 1950s were a period of economic recovery after the war and increasing prosperity for working people. The Prime Minister of the day, Harold Macmillan, was famous for his 'wind of change' speech about decolonisation and independence for the countries of the Empire.

Harold Macmillan

Clement Attlee

Clement Attlee was born in London in 1883. His father was a solicitor and, after studying at Oxford University, Attlee became a barrister. He gave this up to do social work in East London and eventually became a Labour MP.

He was Winston Churchill's Deputy Prime Minister in the wartime coalition government and became Prime Minister after the Labour Party won the 1945 election. He was Prime Minister from 1945 to 1951 and led the Labour Party for 20 years.

Attlee's government undertook the nationalisation of major industries (like coal and steel), created the National Health Service and implemented many of Beveridge's plans for a stronger welfare state. Attlee also introduced measures to improve the conditions of workers.

William Beveridge

William Beveridge (later Lord Beveridge) was a British economist and reformer. He served briefly as a Liberal MP and was subsequently the leade of the Liberals in the House of Lords but is best known for the 1942 report Social Insurance and Allied Services (known as the Beveridge Report).

The report was commissioned by the wartime government in 1941. It recommended that the government should find ways of fighting the five 'Giant Evils' of Want, Disease, Ignorance, Squalor and Idleness and provided the basis of the modern welfare state.

R A Butler

Richard Austen Butler (later Lord Butler) was born in 1902. He became a Conservative MP in 1923 and held several positions before becoming responsible for education in 1941.

In this role, he oversaw the introduction of the Education Act 1944 (often called 'The Butler Act'), which introduced free secondary education in England and Wales. The education system has changed significantly since the Act was introduced, but the division between primary and secondary schools that it enforced still remains in most areas of Britain.

Dylan Thomas

Dylan Thomas was a Welsh poet and writer. He often read and performed his work in public, including for the BBC.

His most well-known works include the radio play Under Milk Wood, first performed after his death in 1954, and the poem Do Not Go Gentle into That Good Night, which he wrote for his dying father in 1952. He died at the age of 39 in New York. There areseveral memorials to him in his birthplace, Swansea, including a statue and the Dylan Thomas Centre.

During the 1950s, there was still a shortage of labour in the UK. Further immigration was therefore encouraged for economic reasons, and many industries advertised for workers from overseas.

For example, centres were set up in the West Indies to recruit people to drive buses. Textile and engineering firms from the north of England and the Midlands sent agents to India and Pakistan to find workers.

For about 25 years, people from the West Indies, India, Pakistan and (later) Bangladesh travelled to work and settle in Britain.

The decade of the 1960s was a period of significant social change. It was known as the 'swinging sixties'. There was growth in British fashion, cinema and popular music. Two well-known pop music groups at the time were The Beatles and The Rolling Stones.

People started to become better off and many bought cars and other consumer goods. It was also a time when social laws were liberalised. The position of women in the workplace also improved.

It was quite common at the time for employers to ask women to leave their jobs when they got married, but Parliament passed new laws giving women the right to equal pay and made it illegal for employers to \ discriminate against women because of their gender.

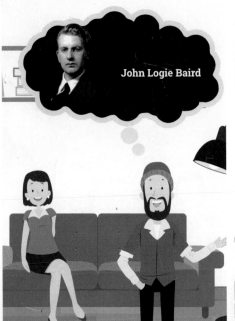

The television was developed by Scotsman John Logie Baird (1888-1946) in the 1920s. In 1932 he made the first television broadcast between London and Glasgow.

A Turing machine is a theoretical mathematical device invented by Alan Turing (1912-54), a British mathematician, in the 1930s. The theory was influential in the development of computer science and the modern-day computer.

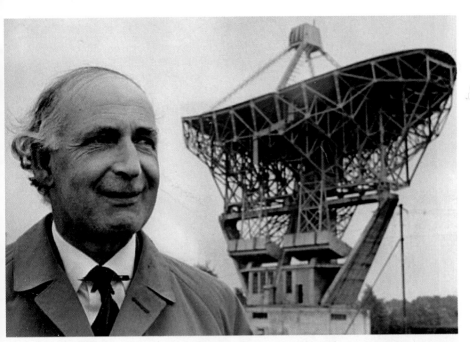

Scotsman Sir Robert Watson-Watt (1892-1973)

Radar was developed by Scotsman Sir Robert Watson-Watt (1892-1973), who proposed that enemy aircraft could be detected by radio waves. The first successful radar test took place in 1935.
Working with radar led Sir Bernard Lovell (1913-2012) to make new discoveries in astronomy. The radio telescope he built at Jodrell Bank in Cheshire was for many years the biggest in the world and continues to operate today.

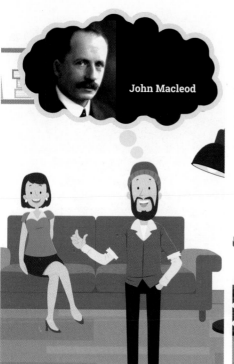

John Macleod

The Scottish physician and researcher John Macleod (1876-1935) was the co-discoverer of insulin, used to treat diabetes.

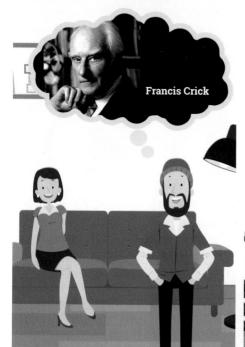

Francis Crick

The structure of the DNA molecule was discovered in 1953 through work at British universities in London and Cambridge. This discovery contributed to many scientific advances, particularly in medicine and fighting crime. Francis Crick (1916-2004), one of those awarded the Nobel Prize for this discovery, was British.

Sir Frank Whittle

The jet engine was developed in Britain in the 1930s by Sir Frank Whittle (1907-96), a British Royal Air Force engineer officer.

Sir Christopher Cockrell

Sir Christopher Cockrell (1910-99), a British inventor, invented the hovercraft in the 1950s.

Britain and France developed Concorde, the world's only supersonic passenger aircraft. It first flew in 1969 and began carrying passengers in 1976. Concorde was retired from service in 2003.

The Harrier jump jet, an aircraft capable of taking off vertically, was also designed and developed in the UK.

James Goodfellow

In the 1960s, James Goodfellow (1937-) invented the cash-dispensing ATM (automatic teller machine) or 'cashpoint'. The first of these was put into use by Barclays Bank in Enfield, north London in 1967.

Sir Robert Edwards

IVF (in-vitro fertilisation) therapy for the treatment of infertility was pioneered in Britain by physiologist Sir Robert Edwards (1925-) and gynaecologist Patrick Steptoe (1913-88). The world's first 'test-tube baby' was born in Oldham, Lancashire in 1978.

Sir Ian Wilmot

In 1996, two British scientists, Sir Ian Wilmot (1944-) and Keith Campbell (1954-2012), led a team which was the first to succeed in cloning a mammal, Dolly the sheep. This has led to further research into the possible use of cloning to preserve endangered species and for medical purposes.

Sir Peter Mansfield

Sir Peter Mansfield (1933-), a British scientist, is the co-inventor of the MRI (magnetic resonance imaging) scanner. This enables doctors and researchers to obtain exact and non-invasive images of human internal organs and has revolutionised diagnostic medicine.

The inventor of the World Wide Web, Sir Tim Berners-Lee (1955-), is British. Information was successfully transferred via the web for the first time on 25 December 1990.

In the late 1970s, the post-war economic boom came to an end. Prices of goods and raw materials began to rise sharply and the exchange rate between the pound and other currencies was unstable. This caused problems with the 'balance of payments': imports of goods were valued at more than the price paid for exports.

Many industries and services were affected by strikes and this caused problems between the trade unions and the government. People began to argue that the unions were too powerful and that their activities were harming the UK.

The 1970s were also a time of serious unrest in Northern Ireland. In 1972, the Northern Ireland Parliament was suspended and Northern Ireland was directly ruled by the UK government. Some 3,000 people lost their lives in the decades after 1969 in the violence of Northern Ireland.

West Germany, France, Belgium, Italy, Luxembourg and the Netherlands formed the European Economic Community (EEC) in 1957. At first the UK did not wish to join the EEC but it eventually did so in 1973. The UK is a full member of the European Union but does not use the Euro currency.

Margaret Thatcher was the daughter of a grocer from Grantham in Lincolnshire. She trained as a chemist and lawyer. She was elected as a Conservative MP in 1959 and became a cabinet minister in 1970 as the Secretary of State for Education and Science. In 1975 she was elected as Leader of the Conservative Party and so became Leader of the Opposition. In 1979, Margaret Thatcher became the first woman Prime Minister of the UK. She was the longest-serving Prime Minister of the 20th century, remaining in office until 1990.

Roald Dahl was born in Wales to Norwegian parents. He served in the Royal Air Force during the Second World War. It was during the 1940s that he began to publish books and short stories. He is most well known for his children's books, although he also wrote for adults. His best-known works include Charlie and the Chocolate Factory and George's Marvellous Medicine. Several of his books have been made into films.

Tony
Blair

In 1997 the Labour Party led by Tony Blair was elected. The Blair government introduced a Scottish Parliament and a Welsh Assembly.
The Scottish Parliament has substantial powers to legislate.

The Welsh Assembly was given fewer legislative powers but considerable control over public services. In Northern Ireland, the Blair government was able to build on the Peace process, resulting in the Good Friday Agreement signed in 1998. The Northern Ireland Assembly was elected in 1999 but suspended in 2002. It was not reinstated until 2007. Most paramilitary groups in Northern Ireland have decommissioned their arms and are inactive. Gordon Brown took over as Prime Minister in 2007.

Throughout the 1990s, Britain played a leading role in coalition forces involved in the liberation of Kuwait, following the Iraqi invasion in 1990, and the conflict in the former Republic of Yugoslavia.

Since 2000, British armed forces have been engaged in the global fight against international terrorism and against the proliferation of weapons of mass destruction, including operations in Afghanistan and Iraq.

Coalition government 2010 onwards In May 2010, and for the first time in the UK since February 1974, no political party won an overall majority in the General Election. The Conservative and Liberal Democrat parties formed a coalition and the leader of the Conservative Party, David Cameron, became Prime Minister.

Brexit is the popular term for the prospective withdrawal of the United Kingdom (UK) from the European Union (EU). In a referendum on 23 June 2016, 51.9% of the participating UK electorate (the turnout was 72.2% of the electorate) voted to leave the EU.

On 29 March 2017, the British government invoked Article 50 of the Treaty on the European Union. The UK is thus on course to leave the EU on 29 March 2019.

On 13 July 2016, two days after becoming Leader of the Conservative Party, May was appointed Prime Minister by Queen Elizabeth II, becoming only the second female British Prime Minister after Margaret Thatcher, and the first female British Prime Minister of the 21st century.

Cities of UK

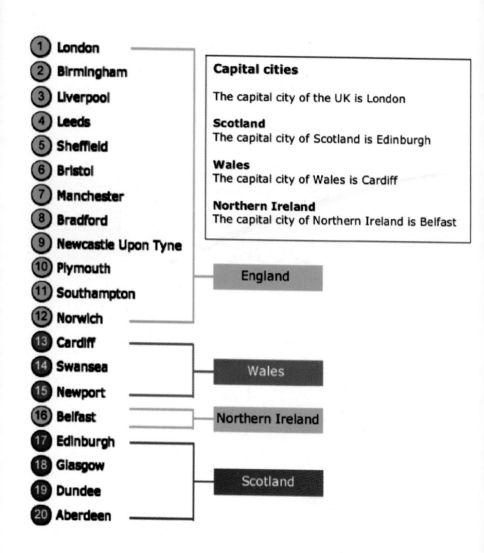

1. London
2. Birmingham
3. Liverpool
4. Leeds
5. Sheffield
6. Bristol
7. Manchester
8. Bradford
9. Newcastle Upon Tyne
10. Plymouth
11. Southampton
12. Norwich
13. Cardiff
14. Swansea
15. Newport
16. Belfast
17. Edinburgh
18. Glasgow
19. Dundee
20. Aberdeen

Capital cities

The capital city of the UK is London

Scotland
The capital city of Scotland is Edinburgh

Wales
The capital city of Wales is Cardiff

Northern Ireland
The capital city of Northern Ireland is Belfast

England

Wales

Northern Ireland

Scotland

UK currency

4 Vector Bank Of England Banknotes © Craig Lowe - www.loweonline.co.uk

The currency in the UK is the pound sterling (symbol £). There are 100 pence in a pound. The denominations (values) of currency are:
Coins: 1p, 2p, 5p, 10p, 20p, 50p, £1 and £2
Notes: £5, £10, £20, £50.

Northern Ireland and Scotland have their own banknotes, which are valid everywhere in the UK. However, shops and businesses do not have to accept them.

There are many variations in language in the different parts of the UK. The English language has many accents and dialects. In Wales, many people speak Welsh – a completely different language from English – and it is taught in schools and universities.

In Scotland, Gaelic (again, a different language) is spoken in some parts of the Highlands and Islands, and in Northern Ireland some people speak Irish Gaelic.

The table below shows how the population of the UK has changed over time.

Population growth in the UK	
Year	**Population**
1600	Just over 4 million
1700	5 million
1801	8 million
1851	20 million
1901	40 million
1951	50 million
1998	57 million
2005	Just under 60 million
2010	Just over 62 million
Source: National Statistics	

Population growth has been faster in more recent years. Migration into the UK and longer life expectancy have played a part in population growth. The population is very unequally distributed over the four parts of the UK. England more or less consistently makes up 84% of the total population, Wales around 5%, Scotland just over 8%, and Northern Ireland less than 3%.

People in the UK are living longer than ever before. This is due to improved living standards and better health care. There are now a record number of people aged 85 and over. This has an impact on the cost of pensions and health care.

The UK population is ethnically diverse and changing rapidly, especially in large cities such as London. It is not always easy to get an exact picture of the ethnic origin of all the population. There are people in the UK with ethnic origins from all over the world.

In surveys, the most common ethnic description chosen is white, which includes people of European, Australian, Canadian, New Zealand and American descent. Other significant groups are those of Asian, black and mixed descent.

Women in Britain today make up about half of the workforce. On average, girls leave school with better qualifications than boys. More women than men study at university.

The UK is historically a Christian country. In the 2009 Citizenship Survey, 70% of people identified themselves as Christian. Much smaller proportions identified themselves as Muslim (4%), Hindu (2%), Sikh (1%), Jewish or Buddhist (both less than 0.5%), and 2% of people followed another religion. There are religious buildings for other religions all over the UK. This includes Islamic mosques, Hindu temples, Jewish synagogues, Sikh gurdwaras and Buddhist temples. However, everyone has the legal right to choose their religion, or to choose not to practise a religion. In the Citizenship Survey, 21% of people said that they had no religion.

In England, there is a constitutional link between Church and state. The official Church of the state is the Church of England (called the Anglican Church in other countries and the Episcopal Church in Scotland and the United States). The monarch is the head of the Church of England. The spiritual leader of the Church of England is the Archbishop of Canterbury.

In Scotland, the national Church is the Church of Scotland, which is a Presbyterian Church. It is governed by ministers and elders. The chairperson of the General Assembly of the Church of Scotland is the Moderator, who is appointed for one year only and often speaks on behalf of that Church. There is no established Church in Wales or Northern Ireland.

England, Scotland, Wales and Northern Ireland each have a national saint, called a patron saint. Each saint has a special day:
• 1 March: St David's Day, Wales
• 17 March: St Patrick's Day, Northern Ireland
• 23 April: St George's Day, England
• 30 November: St Andrew's Day, Scotland.
Only Scotland and Northern Ireland have their patron saint's day as an official holiday (although in Scotland not all businesses and offices will close). Events are held across Scotland, Northern Ireland and the rest of the country, especially where there are a lot of people of Scottish, Northern Irish and Irish heritage.

Christmas Day, 25 December, celebrates the birth of Jesus Christ. It is a public holiday. Many Christians go to church on Christmas Eve (24 December) or on Christmas Day itself. Christmas is celebrated in a traditional way. People usually spend the day at home and eat a special meal, which often includes roast turkey, Christmas pudding and mince pies. They give gifts, send cards and decorate their houses. Christmas is a special time for children. Very young children believe that Father Christmas (also known as Santa Claus) brings them presents during the night before Christmas Day. Many people decorate a tree in their home.

Boxing Day is the day after Christmas Day and is a public holiday.

Easter takes place in March or April. It marks the death of Jesus Christ on Good Friday and his rising from the dead on Easter Sunday. Both Good Friday and the following Monday, called Easter Monday, are public holidays. Easter is also celebrated by people who are not religious. 'Easter eggs' are chocolate eggs given as presents as a symbol of new life.

The 40 days before Easter are known as Lent. It is a time when Christians take time to reflect and prepare for Easter. Traditionally, people would fast during this period and today many people will give something up, like a favourite food. The day before Lent starts is called Shrove Tuesday, or Pancake Day. People eat pancakes, which were traditionally made to use up foods such as eggs, fat and milk before fasting. Lent begins on Ash Wednesday. There are church services where Christians are marked with an ash cross on their forehead as a symbol of death and sorrow for sin.

Diwali normally falls in October or November and lasts for five days. It is often called the Festival of Lights. It is celebrated by Hindus and Sikhs. It celebrates the victory of good over evil and the gaining of knowledge. There are different stories about how the festival came about. There is a famous celebration of Diwali in Leicester.
Diwali is popularly known as the **Festival of Lights.**

Hannukah

Hannukah is in November or December and is celebrated for eight days. It is to remember the Jews' struggle for religious freedom. On each day of the festival a candle is lit on a stand of eight candles (called a menorah) to remember the story of the festival, where oil that should have lasted only a day did so for eight.

Eid a-Fitr celebrates the end of Ramadan, when Muslims have fasted for a month. They thank Allah for giving them the strength to complete the fast. The date when it takes place changes every year. Muslims attend special services and meals.

Eid ul Adha remembers that the prophet Ibrahim was willing to sacrifice his son when God ordered him to . It reminds Muslims of their own commitment to God. Many Muslims sacrifice an animal to eat during this festival. In Britain this has to be done in a slaughterhouse.

New Year, 1 January, is a public holiday. People usually celebrate on the night of 31 December (called New Year's Eve). In Scotland, 31 December is called Hogmanay and 2 January is also a public holiday. For some Scottish people, Hogmanay is a bigger holiday than Christmas.

Vaisakhi

Vaisakhi (also spelled Baisakhi) is a Sikh festival which celebrates the founding of the Sikh community known as the Khalsa. It is celebrated on 14 April each year with parades, dancing and singing.

April Fool's Day, 1 April, is a day when people play jokes on each other until midday. The television and newspapers often have stories that are April Fool jokes.

Valentine's Day, 14 February, is when lovers exchange cards and gifts. Sometimes people send anonymous cards to someone they secretly admire.

Father's Day is the third Sunday in June. Children send cards or buy gifts for their fathers.

Mothering Sunday (or Mother's day) is the Sunday three weeks before Easter. Children send cards or buy gifts for their mothers.

Halloween, 31 October, is an ancient festival and has roots in the pagan festival to mark the beginning of winter. Young people will often dress up in frightening costumes to play 'trick or treat'. People give them treats to stop them playing tricks on them. A lot of people carve lanterns out of pumpkins and put a candle inside of them.

Bonfire Night, 5 November, is an occasion when people in Great Britain set off fireworks at home or in special displays. The origin of this celebration was an event in 1605, when a group of Catholics led by Guy Fawkes failed in their plan to kill the Protestant king with a bomb in the Houses of Parliament.

Remembrance Day, 11 November, commemorates those who died fighting for the UK and its allies. Originally it commemorated the dead of the First World War, which ended on 11 November 1918. People wear poppies (the red flower found on the battlefields of the First World War). At 11.00 am there is a two-minute silence and wreaths are laid at the Cenotaph in Whitehall, London.

As well as those mentioned previously, there are other public holidays each year called bank holidays, when banks and many other businesses are closed for the day. These are of no religious significance. They are at the beginning of May in late May or early June, and in August. In Northern Ireland, the anniversary of the Battle of the Boyne in July is also a public holiday.

BANK HOLIDAY

Zaina now I will brief you about all the Leisure Activities of UK.

Sir Roger Bannister

Sir Roger Bannister (1929-) was the first man in the world to run a mile in under four minutes, in 1954.

Sir Jackie Stewart (1939-) is a Scottish former racing driver who won the Formula 1 world championship three times.

Sporting events take place at major stadiums such as Wembley Stadium in London and the Millennium Stadium in Cardiff. The UK has hosted the Olympic games on three occasions: 1908, 1948 and 2012. The main Olympic site for the 2012 Games was in Stratford, East London. The British team was very successful, across a wide range of Olympic sports, finishing third in the medal table.

The Paralympic Games for 2012 were also hosted in London. The Paralympics have their origin in the work of Dr Sir Ludwig Guttman, a German refugee, at the Stoke Mandeville hospital in Buckinghamshire. Dr Guttman developed new methods of treatment for people with spinal injuries and encouraged patients to take part in exercise and sport.

Bobby
Moore

Bobby Moore (1941-93) captained the English football team that won the World Cup in 1966.

Sir Ian
Botham

Sir Ian Botham (1955-) captained the English cricket team and holds a number of English Test cricket records, both for batting and for bowling.

Jayne Torvill (1957) and Christopher Dean (1958-) won gold medals for ice dancing at the Olympic Games in 1984 and is one of Britain's greatest Olympians.

Sir Steve Redgrave (1962-) won gold medals in rowing in five consecutive Olympic Games and is one of Britain's greatest Olympians.

Baroness Tanni Grey-Thompson

Baroness Tanni Grey-Thompson (1969-) is an athlete who uses a wheelchair and won 16 Paralympic medals, including 11 gold medals, in races over five Paralympic Games. She won the London Marathon six times and broke a total of 30 world records.

Dame Kelly Holmes

Dame Kelly Holmes (1970) won two gold medals for running in the 2004 Olympic Games. She has held a number of British and European records.

Dame Ellen MacArthur

Dame Ellen MacArthur (1976-) is a yachts woman and in 2004 became the fastest person to sail around the world single handed.

Sir Chris Hoy

Sir Chris Hoy (1976-) is a Scottish cyclist who has won six gold and one silver Olympic medals. He has also won 11 world championship titles.

David Weir

David Weir (1979-) is a Paralympian who uses a wheelchair and has won six gold medals over two Paralympic Games. He has also won the London Marathon six times.

Bradley Wiggins

Bradley Wiggins (1980-) is a cyclist. In 2012, he became the first Briton to win the Tour de France. He has won seven Olympic Medals, including gold medals in the 2004, 2008 and 2012 Olympic Games.

Mo Farah

Mo Farah (1983-) is a British distance runner, born in Somalia. He won gold medals in the 2012 Olympics for the 5,000 and 10,000 metres and is the first Briton to win the Olympic gold medal in the 10,000 metres.

Jessica Ennis

Jessica Ennis (1986-) is an athlete. She won the 2012 Olympic gold medal in the heptathlon, which includes seven different track and field events. She also holds a number of British athletics records.

Andy Murray

Andy Murray (1987-) is a Scottish tennis player who in 2012 won the men's singles in the US Open. He is the first British man to win a singles title in a Grand Slam tournament since 1936. In the same year, he won Olympic gold and silver medals and was runner-up in the men's singles at Wimbledon

Ellie Simmonds

Ellie Simmonds (1994-) is a Paralympian who won gold medals for swimming at the 2008 and 2012 Paralympic Games and holds a number of world records. She was the youngest member of the British team at the 2008 Games.

Cricket originated in England and is now played in many countries. Games can last up to five days but still result in a draw! The idiosyncratic nature of the game and its complex laws are said to reflect the best of the British character and sense of fair play. You may come across expressions such as 'rain stopped play', 'batting on a sticky wicket', 'playing a straight bat', 'bowled a googly' or 'it's just not cricket', which have passed into everyday usage. The most famous competition is the Ashes, which is a series of Test matches played between England and Australia.

Football

Football is the UK's most popular sport. It has a long history in the UK and the first professional football clubs were formed in the late 19th century.

Rugby originated in England in the early 19th century and is very popular in the UK today. The most famous rugby union competition is the Six Nations Championship between England, Ireland, Scotland, Wales, France and Italy. The Super League is the most well-known rugby league (club) competition.

The modern game of golf can be traced back to 15th century Scotland. It is a popular sport played socially as well as professionally. There are public and private golf courses all over the UK. St Andrews in Scotland is known as the home of golf.

The open championship is the only 'Major' tournament held outside the United States. It is hosted by a different golf course every year.

Tennis

Modern tennis evolved in England in the late 19th century. The first tennis club was founded in Leamington Spa in 1872. The most famous tournament hosted in Britain is The Wimbledon Championships, which takes place each year at the All England Lawn Tennis and Croquet Club. It is the oldest tennis tournament in the world and the only 'Grand Slam' event played on grass.

Sir Francis Chichester

A British sailor, Sir Francis Chichester, was the first person to sail singlehanded around the world, in 1966/67. Two years later, Sir Robin Knox-Johnston became the first person to do this without stopping. Rowing is also popular, both as a leisure activity and as a competitive sport. There is a popular yearly race on the Thames between Oxford and Cambridge Universities.

Motor Sport

There is a long history of motor sport in the UK, for both cars and motor cycles. Motor-car racing in the UK started in 1902. The UK continues to be a world leader in the development and manufacture of motor-sport technology. A Formula 1 Grand Prix event is held in the UK each year and a number of British Grand Prix drivers have won the Formula 1 World Championship. Recent British winners include Damon Hill, Lewis Hamilton and Jenson Button.

Skiing
Skiing is increasingly popular in the UK. Many people go abroad to ski and there are also dry slopes throughout the UK. Skiing on snow may also be possible during the winter. There are five ski centres in Scotland, as well as Europe's longest dry ski slope near Edinburgh.

Zaina now we are moving on to "Art and Culture.'

The Proms is an eight-week summer season of orchestral classical music that takes place in various venues, including the Royal Albert Hall in London. It has been in various venues, including the Royal Albert Hall in London. It has been organised by the British Broadcasting Corporation (BBC) since 1927. The Last Night of the Proms is the most well-known concert and (along with others in the series) is broadcast on television.

Henry Purcell

Henry Purcell (1659-95) was the organist at Westminster Abbey. He wrote church music, operas and other pieces, and developed a British style distinct from that elsewhere in Europe.

George Frederick Handel

The German-born composer George Frederick Handel (1685-1759) spent many years in the UK and became a British citizen in 1727. He wrote the Water Music for King George I and Music for the Royal Fireworks for his son, George II. Both these pieces continue to be very popular. Handel also wrote an oratorio, Messiah, which is sung regularly by choirs, often at Easter time.

Gustav Holst

Gustav Holst (1874-1934), whose work includes The Planets, a suite of pieces themed around the planets and the solar system. He adapted Jupiter, part of the Planets suite, as the tune for I owe to thee my country, a popular hymn in British churches.

Sir Edward Elgar

Sir Edward Elgar (1857-1934) was born in Worcester, England. His best known work is probably the Pomp and Circumstance Marches. March No1 (Land of Hope and Glory) is usually played at the Last Night of the Proms at the Royal Albert Hall.

Ralph
Vaughan
Williams

Ralph Vaughan Williams (1872-1958) wrote music for orchestras and choirs. He was strongly influenced by traditional English folk music.

Sir William Walton

Sir William Walton (1902-83) wrote a wide range of music, from film scores to opera. He wrote marches for the coronations of King George VI and Queen Elizabeth II but his best-known works are probably Façade, which became a ballet, and Balthazar's Feast, which is intended to be sung by a large choir.

Benjamin Britten

Benjamin Britten (1913-76) is best known for his operas, which include Peter Grimes and Billy Budd. He also wrote A Young Person's Guide to the Orchestra, which is based on a piece of music by Purcell and introduces the listener to the various different sections of an orchestra. He founded the Aldeburgh festival in Suffolk, which continues to be a popular music event of international importance.

Mercury Music Prize

The Mercury Music Prize is awarded each September for the best album from the UK and Ireland. The Brit Awards is an annual event that gives awards in a range of categories, such as best British group and best British solo artist.

There are theatres in most towns and cities throughout the UK, ranging from the large to the small. They are an important part of local communities and often show both professional and amateur productions.

London's west end, also known as 'Theatreland', is particularly well known. The Mousetrap, a murder-mystery play by Dame Agatha Christie, has been running in the west end since 1952 and has had the longest initial run of any show in history.

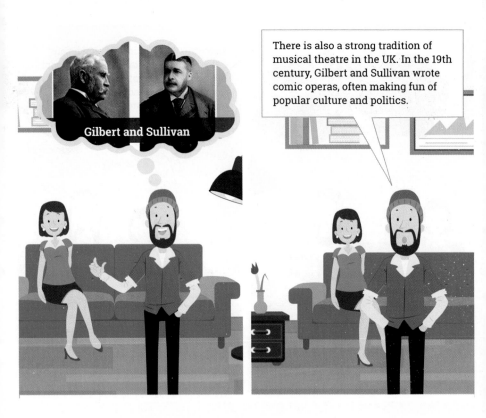

There is also a strong tradition of musical theatre in the UK. In the 19th century, Gilbert and Sullivan wrote comic operas, often making fun of popular culture and politics.

Gilbert and Sullivan

These operas include HMS Pinafore, The Pirates of Penzance and The Mikado. Gilbert and Sullivan's work is still often staged by professional and amateur groups. More recently, Andrew Lloyd Webber has written the music for shows which have been popular throughout the world, including, in collaboration with Tim Rice, Jesus Christ Superstar and Evita, and also Cats and The Phantom of the Opera.

One British tradition is the pantomime. Many theatres produce a pantomime at Christmas time. They are based on fairy stories and are light-hearted plays with music and comedy, enjoyed by family audiences. One of the traditional characters is the Dame, a woman played by a man. There is often also a pantomime horse or cow played by two actors in the same costume.

The Edinburgh Festival takes place in Edinburgh, Scotland, every summer. It is a series of different arts and cultural festivals, with the biggest and most well-known being the Edinburgh Festival Fringe ('the Fringe'). The Fringe is a showcase of mainly theatre and comedy performances. It often shows experimental work.

The Laurence Olivier Awards take place annually at different venues in London. There are a variety of categories, including best director, best actor and best actress. The awards are named after the British actor Sir Laurence Olivier, late Lord Olivier, who was best known for his roles in various Shakespeare plays.

Sir Anthony Van Dyck

Many of the painters working in Britain in the 16th and 17th centuries were from abroad-for example, Hans Holbein and Sir Anthony Van Dyck.

Works by British and international artists are displayed in Galleries across the UK. Some of the most well-known galleries are The National Gallery, Tate Britain and Tate Modern in London, the National Museum in Cardiff, and the National Gallery of Scotland in Edinburgh.

The Turner Prize was established in 1984 and celebrates contemporary art. It was named after Joseph Turner. Four works are shortlisted every year and shown at Tate Britain before the winner is announced. The Turner Prize is recognised as one of the most prestigious visual art awards in Europe. Previous winners include Damien Hirst and Richard Wright.

Thomas Gainsborough (1727-88) was a portrait painter who often painted people in country or garden scenery.

David Allan (1744-96) was a Scottish painter who was best known for painting portraits. One of his most famous works is called The Origin of Painting.

Joseph Turner (1775-1851) was an influential landscape painter in a modern style. He is considered the artist who raised the profile of landscape painting.

John Constable (1776-1837) was a landscape painter most famous for his works of Dedham Vale on the Suffolk-Essex border in the east of England.

The Pre-Raphaelites were an important group of artists in the second half of the 19th century. They painted detailed pictures on religious or literary themes in bright colours. The group included Holman Hunt, Dante Gabriel Rossetti and Sir John Millais.

Sir John Lavery (1856-1941) was a very successful Northern Irish portrait painter. His work included painting the Royal Family.

Henry Moore (1898-1986) was an English sculptor and artist. He is best known for his large bronze abstract sculptures.

John Petts

John Petts (1914-91) was a Welsh artist, best known for his engravings and stained glass.

Lucian Freud

Lucian Freud (1922-2011) was a German-born British artist. He is best known for his portraits.

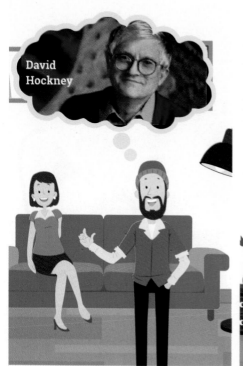

David Hockney (1937-) was an important contributor to the 'pop art' movement of the 1960s and continues to be influential today.

In the Middle Ages, great cathedrals and churches were built, many of which still stand today. Examples are the cathedrals in Durham, Lincoln, Canterbury and Salisbury. The White Tower in the Tower of London is an example of a Norman castle keep, built on the orders of William the Conqueror.

In the 18th century, simpler designs became popular. The Scottish architect Robert Adam influenced the development of architecture in the UK, Europe and America. He designed the inside decoration as well as the building itself in great houses such as Dumfries House in Scotland. His ideas influenced architects in cities such as Bath, where the Royal Crescent was built.

In the 19th century, the medieval 'gothic' style became popular again. As cities expanded, many great public buildings were built in this style. The Houses of Parliament and St Pancras Station were built at this time, as were the town halls in cities such as Manchester and Sheffield.

Sir Edwin Lutyens

In the 20th century, Sir Edwin Lutyens had an influence throughout the British Empire. He designed New Delhi to be the seat of government in India.

The Cenotaph

After the First World War, Sir Edwin Lutyenswas responsible for many war memorials throughout the world, including the Cenotaph in Whitehall. The Cenotaph is the site of the annual Remembrance Day service attended by the Queen, politicians and foreign ambassadors.

Modern British architects including Sir Norman Foster, Lord (Richard) Rogers and Dame Zaha Hadid continue to work on major projects throughout the world as well as within the UK.

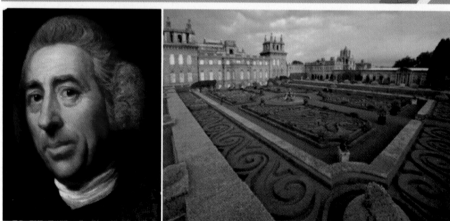

Alongside the development of architecture, garden design and landscaping have played an important role in the UK. In the 18th century, Lancelot 'Capability' Brown designed the grounds around country houses so that the landscape appeared to be natural, with grass, trees and lakes. He often said that a place had 'capabilities'. Later, Gertrude Jekyll often worked with worked with Edwin Lutyens to design colourful gardens around the houses he designed. Gardens continue to be an important part of homes in the UK. The annual Chelsea Flower Show showcases garden design from Britain and around the world.

Britain has produced many great designers, from Thomas Chippendale (who designed furniture in the 18th century) to Clarice Cliff (who designed Art Deco ceramics) to Sir Terence Conran (a 20th-century interior designer).

Leading fashion designers of recent years include Mary Quant, Alexander McQueen and Vivienne Westwood.

The UK has a prestigious literary history and tradition. Several British writers, including the novelist Sir William Golding, the poet Seamus Heaney, and the playwright Harold Pinter, have won the Nobel Prize in Literature.

Other authors have become well known in popular fiction. Agatha Christie's detective stories are read all over the world and Ian Fleming's books introduced James Bond. In 2003, The Lord of the Rings by JRR Tolkien was voted the country's best-loved novel.

The Man Booker Prize for Fiction is awarded annually for the best fiction novel written by an author from the Commonwealth, Ireland or Zimbabwe. It has been awarded since 1968. Past winners include Ian McEwan, Hilary Mantel and Julian Barnes.

Jane Austen

Jane Austen (1775-1817) was an English novelist. Her books include Pride and Prejudice and Sense and Sensibility. Her novels are concerned with marriage and family relationships. Many have been made into television programmes or films.

Charles Dickens

Charles Dickens (1812-70) wrote a number of very famous novels, including Oliver twist and Great Expectations. You will hear references in everyday talk to some of the characters in his books, such as Scrooge (a mean person) or Mr Micawber (always hopeful).

Thomas Hardy

Thomas Hardy (1840-1928) was an author and poet. His best-known novels focus on rural society and include Far from the Madding Crowd and Jude the Obscure.

Sir Arthur Conan Doyle

Sir Arthur Conan Doyle (1859-1930) was a Scottish doctor and writer. He was best known for his stories about Sherlock Holmes, who was one of the first fictional detectives.

Robert Louis Stevenson (1850-94) wrote books which are still read by adults and children today. His most famous books include Treasure Island, Kidnapped and Dr Jekyll and Mr Hyde.

Evelyn Waugh (1903-66) wrote satirical novels, including Decline and Fall and Scoop. He is perhaps best known for Brideshead Revisited.

Sir Kingsley Amis (1922-95) was an English novelist and poet. He wrote more than 20 novels. The most well known is Lucky Jim.

Graham Greene (1904-91) wrote novels often influenced by his religious beliefs, including The Heart of the Matter, The Honorary Consul, Brighton Rock and Our Man in Havana.

J K Rowling

J K Rowling (1965-) wrote the Harry Potter series of children's books, which have enjoyed huge international success. She now writes fiction for adults as well.

The Anglo-Saxon poem Beowulf tells of its hero's battles against monsters and is still translated into modern English. Poems which survive from the Middle Ages include Chaucer's Canterbury Tales and a poem called Sir Gawain and the Green Knight, about one of the knights at the court of King Arthur.

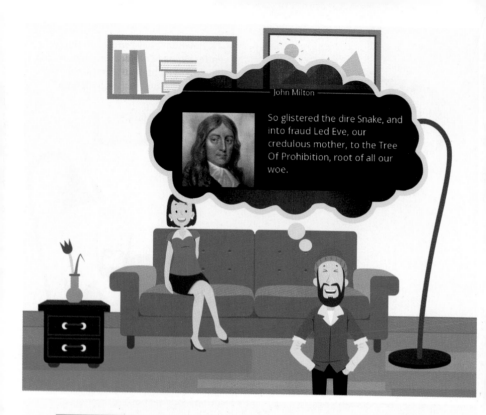

As well as plays, Shakespeare wrote many sonnets (poems which must be 14 lines long) and some longer poems. As Protestant ideas spread, a number of poets wrote poems inspired by their religious views. One of these was John Milton, who wrote Paradise Lost.

Other poets, including William Wordsworth, were inspired by nature. Sir Walter Scott wrote poems inspired by Scotland and the traditional stories and songs from the area on the borders of Scotland and England. He also wrote novels, many of which were set in Scotland.

Poetry was very popular in the 19th century, with poets such as William Blake, John Keats, Lord Byron, Percy Shelley, Alfred Lord Tennyson, and Robert and Elizabeth Browning.

Later, many poets-for example, Wilfred Owen and Siegfried Sassoon – were inspired to write about their experiences in the First World War. More recently, popular poets have included Sir Walter de la Mare, John Masefield, Sir John Betjeman and Ted Hughes. Some of the best-known poets are buried or commemorated in Poet's Corner in Westminster Abbey.

Some famous lines include:

'Oh, to be in England now that April's there, And whoever wakes in England sees, some morning, unaware, That the lowest boughs and the brushwood sheaf Round the elm-tree bole are in tiny leaf, While the Chaffinch sings on the orchard bough In England – Now!'

Robert Browning

Robert Browning, 1812-89 –
Home Thoughts from Abroad.
Some famous lines include:
- 'Oh, to be in England now that April's there And whoever wakes in England sees, some morning, unaware, That the lowest boughs and the brushwood sheaf
- Round the elm-tree bole are in tiny leaf While the Chaffinch sings on the orchard bough, In England – Now!'

Lord Byron

Lord Byron, 1788-1824 –
She walks in Beauty
'She walks in beauty, like the night Of cloudless climes and starry skies, All that's best of dark and bright Meet in her aspect and her eyes'

William Blake, 1757-1827 – **The Tyger**
'Tyger! Tyger! Burning bright
In the forests of the night,
What immortal hand and eye
Could frame thy fearful symmetry?'

Wilfred Owen, 1893-1918 –
Anthem for Doomed Youth
'What passing-bells for these who die
as cattle?
Only the monstrous anger of the guns.
Only the stuttering rifles' rapid rattle
Can patter out their hasty orisons.'

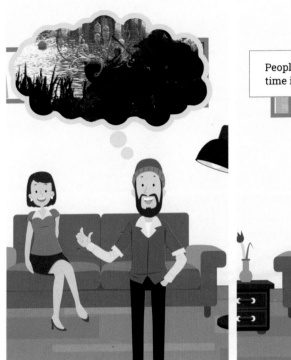

People in the UK spend their leisure time in many different ways.

Gardening
A lot of people have gardens at home and will spend their free time looking after them. Some people rent additional land called 'an allotment', where they grow fruit and vegetables. Gardening and flower shows range from major national exhibitions to small local events.

Kew Gardens

Bodnant Garden

Mount Stewart gardens

Crathes Castle garden

Many towns have garden centres selling plants and gardening equipment. There are famous gardens to visit throughout the UK, including Kew Gardens, Sissinghurst and Hidcote in England, Crathes Castle and Inveraray Castle in Scotland, Bodnant Garden in Wales, and Mount Stewart in Northern Ireland.

Shopping
There are many different places to go shopping in the UK. Most towns and cities have a central shopping area, which is called the town centre.

Undercover shopping centres are also common – these might be in town centres or on the outskirts of a town or city. Most shops in the UK are open seven days a week, although trading hours on Sundays and public holidays are generally reduced. Many towns also have markets on one or more days a week, where stallholders sell a variety of goods.

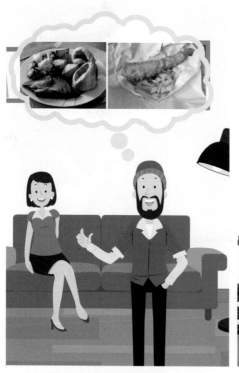

England: Roast beef, which is served with potatoes, vegetables, Yorkshire puddings (batter that is baked in the oven) and other accompaniments. Fish and chips are also popular.

Scotland:
Haggis – a sheep's stomach stuffed with offal. Suet, onions and oatmeal.

Northern Ireland: Ulster fry – a fried meal with bacon, eggs, sausage, black pudding, tomatoes, mushrooms, soda bread and potato bread.

Wales: welsh cakes – traditional Welsh snack made from flour, dried fruits and spices, and served either hot or cold.

The UK has had a major influence on modern cinema.
Films were first shown publicly in the UK in 1896 and film screenings very quickly became popular. From the beginning, British film makers became famous for clever special effects and this continues to be an area of British expertise.

Sir Charles (Charlie) Chaplin

Sir Charles (Charlie) Chaplin became famous in silent movies for his tramp character and was one of many British actors to make a career in Hollywood.

British studios flourished in the 1930s. Eminent directors included Sir Alexander Korda and Sir Alfred Hitchcock, who later left for Hollywood and remained an important film director until his death in 1980. During the Second World War, British movies (for example, In Which We Serve) played an important part in boosting morale. Later, British directors including Sir David Lean and Ridley Scott found great success both in the UK and internationally.

The 1950s and 1960s were a high point for British comedies, including Passport to Pimlico, The Ladykilllers and, later, the Carry On Films.

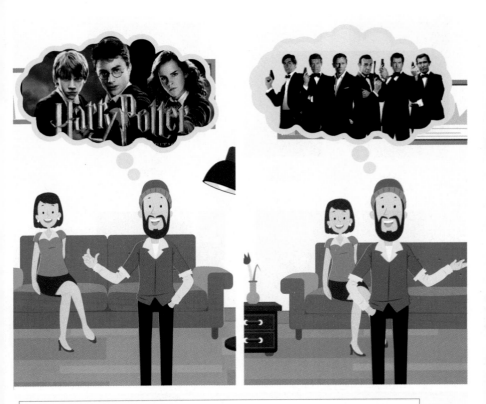

Many of the films now produced in the UK are made by foreign companies, using British expertise. Some of the most commercially successful films of all time, including the two highest-grossing film franchises (Harry Potter and James Bond), have been produced in the UK. Ealing Studios has a claim to being the oldest continuously working film studio facility in the world. Britain continues to be particularly strong in special effects and animation. One example is the work of Nick Park, who has won four Oscars for his animated films, including three for films featuring Wallace and Gromit.

Kate
Winslet

Tilda
Swinton

Dame Judi
Dench

Sir Anthony
Hopkins

Colin
Firth

Actors such as Sir Lawrence Olivier, David Niven, Sir Rex Harrison and Richard Burton starred in a wide variety of popular films. British actors continue to be popular and continue to win awards throughout the world. Recent British actors to have won Oscars include Colin Firth, Sir Antony Hopkins, Dame Judi Dench, Kate Winslet and Tilda Swinton.

The annual British Academy Film Awards, hosted by the British Academy of Film and Television Arts (BAFTA), are the British equivalent of the Oscars.

The 39 Steps (1935), directed by Alfred Hitchcock

Brief Encounter (1945), directed by David Lean

The Third Man (1949), directed by Carol Reed

Don't Look Now (1973), directed by Nicolas Roeg

Chariots of Fire (1981), directed by Hugh Hudson

The Killing Fields (1984), directed by Roland Joffé

The Belles of St Trinian's (1954), directed by Frank Launder

Lawrence of Arabia (1962), directed by David Lean

Women in Love (1969), directed by Ken Russell

Four Weddings and a Funeral (1994), directed by Mike Newell

Touching the Void (2003), directed by Kevin MacDonald.

The traditions of comedy and satire, and the ability to laugh at ourselves, are an important part of the UK character.

In the 19th century, satirical magazines began to be published. The most famous was Punch, which was published for the first time in the 1840s. Today, political cartoons continue to be published in newspapers, and magazines such as Private Eye continue the tradition of satire.

Comedians were a popular feature of British music hall, a form of variety theatre which was very common until television became the leading form of entertainment in the UK. Some of the people who had performed in the music halls in the 1940s and 1950s, such as Morecambe and Wise, became stars of television.

Television comedy developed its own style. Situation comedies, or sitcoms, which often look at family life and relationships in the workplace, remain popular. Satire has also continued to be important, with shows like That Was The Week That Was in the 1960s and Spitting Image in the 1980s and 1990s. In 1969, Monty Python's Flying Circus introduced a new type of progressive comedy. Stand-up comedy, where a solo comedian talks to a live audience, has become popular again in recent years.

Many different television (TV) channels are available in the UK. Some are free to watch a wide variety of programmes. Popular programmes include regular soap operas such as Coronation Street and EastEnders.

Social networking websites such as Facebook and Twitter are a popular way for people to stay in touch with friends, organise social events, and share photos, videos and opinions. Many people use social networking on their mobile phones when out and about.

Public houses (pubs) are an important part of the UK social culture. Pubs are usually open during the day from 11.00 am (12 noon on Sundays). To buy alcohol in a pub or night club you must be 18 or over, but people under that age may be allowed in some pubs with an adult. When they are 16, people can drink wine or beer with a meal in a hotel or restaurant (including eating areas in pubs) as long as they are with someone over 18.

In the UK, people often enjoy a gamble on sports or other events. There are also casinos in many places. You have to be 18 to go into betting shops or gambling clubs.

There is a National Lottery for which draws are made every week. You can enter by buying a ticket or a scratch card. People under 16 are not allowed to participate in the National Lottery.

A lot of people in the UK have pets such as cats or dogs. They might have them for company or because they enjoy looking after them. It is against the law to treat a pet cruelly or to neglect it. All dogs in public places must wear a collar showing the name and address of the owner. The owner is responsible for keeping the dog under control and for cleaning up after the animal in a public place.

The countries that make up the UK all have flowers which are particularly associated with them and which are sometimes worn on national saints' days:
- England – the rose
- Scotland – the thistle
- Wales – the daffodil
- Northern Ireland – the shamrock.

Zaina here we finish "Leisure".
Next topic is "Places of Interest", let's move out.

Sounds Great.
I am ready, let's go.

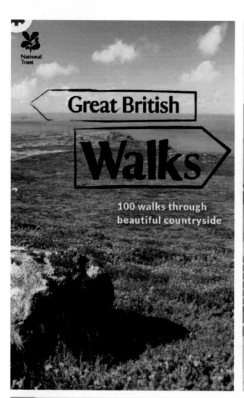

Great British **Walks**

100 walks through
beautiful countryside

The UK has a large network of public footpaths in the countryside. There are also many opportunities for mountain biking, mountaineering and hill walking. There are 15 national parks in England, Wales and Scotland. They are areas of protected countryside that everyone can visit, and where people live, work and look after the landscape.

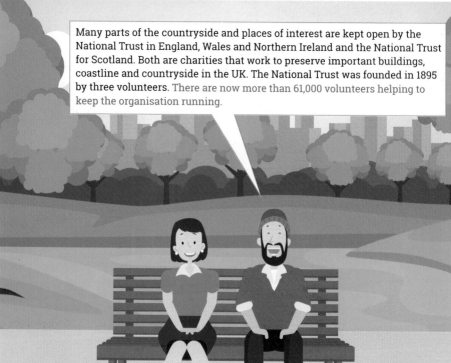

Many parts of the countryside and places of interest are kept open by the National Trust in England, Wales and Northern Ireland and the National Trust for Scotland. Both are charities that work to preserve important buildings, coastline and countryside in the UK. The National Trust was founded in 1895 by three volunteers. There are now more than 61,000 volunteers helping to keep the organisation running.

That's Big Ben Clock
Big Ben is the nickname for the great bell of the clock at the House of Parliament in London. Many people call the clock Big Ben as well. The clock is over 150 years old and is a popular tourist attraction. The clock is named 'Elizabeth Tower' in honour of Queen Elizabeth II's Diamond Jubilee in 2012.

The Eden Project
The Eden Project is located in Cornwall, in the south west of England. Its biomes, which are like giant greenhouses, house plants from all over the world.

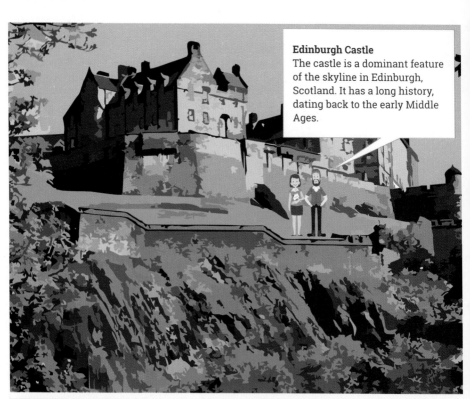

Edinburgh Castle
The castle is a dominant feature of the skyline in Edinburgh, Scotland. It has a long history, dating back to the early Middle Ages.

The Giant's Causeway
Located on the north-east coast of Northern Ireland, the Giant's Causeway is a land formation of columns made from volcanic lava. It was formed about 50 million years ago. There are many legends about the Causeway and how it was formed.

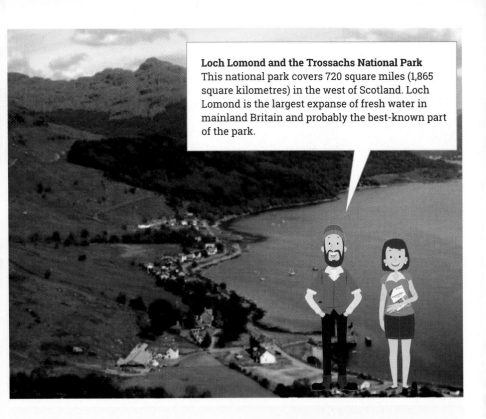

Loch Lomond and the Trossachs National Park
This national park covers 720 square miles (1,865 square kilometres) in the west of Scotland. Loch Lomond is the largest expanse of fresh water in mainland Britain and probably the best-known part of the park.

London Eye
The London Eye is situated on the southern bank of the River Thames and is a Ferris wheel that is 443 feet (135 metres) tall. It was originally built as part of the UK's celebration of the new millennium and continues to be an important part of New Year celebrations.

The Tower of London
The Tower of London was first built by William the Conqueror after he became king in 1066. Tours are given by the Yeoman Warders, also known as Beefeaters, who tell visitors about the building's history. People can also see the Crown Jewels there.

The Lake District
The Lake District is England's largest national park. It covers 885 square miles (2,292 square kilometres). It is famous for its lakes and mountains and is very popular with climbers, walkers and sailors. The biggest stretch of water is Windermere. In 2007, television viewers voted Wastwater as Britain's favourite view.

It's so beautiful here. So romantic. Love it

Democracy is a system of government where the whole adult population gets a say. This might be by direct voting or by choosing representatives to make decisions on their behalf.

At the turn of the 19th century, Britain was not a democracy as we know it today. Although there were elections to select members of Parliament (Mps), only a small group of people could vote. They were men who were over 21 years of age and who owned a certain amount of property.

The franchise (that is the number of people who had the right to vote) grew over the course of the 19th century and political parties began to involve ordinary men and women as members.

In the 1830s and 1840s, a group called the Chartists campaigned for reform. They wanted six changes: for every man to have the vote, elections every year, for all regions to be equal in the electoral system, secret ballots, for any man to be able to stand as an MP, for MPs to be paid.

At the time, the campaign was generally seen as failure. However, by 1918 most of these reforms had been adopted. The voting franchise was also extended to women over 30, and then in 1928 to men and women over 21. In 1969, the voting age was reduced to 18 for men and women.

A constitution is a set of principles by which a country is governed. It includes all of the institutions that are responsible for running the country and how their power is kept in check. The constitution also includes laws and conventions. The British constitution is not written down in any single document, and therefore it is described as 'unwritten'.

Constitutional institutions

In the UK, there are several different parts of government.
The main ones are:
- the monarchy
- Parliament (the House of Commons and the House of Lords)
- the Prime Minister
- the cabinet
- the judiciary (courts)
- the police
- the civil service
- local government.

In addition, there are devolved governments in Scotland, Wales and Northern Ireland that have the power to legislate on certain issues.

Queen Elizabeth II

Queen Elizabeth II is the head of state of the UK. She is also the monarch or head of state for many countries in the Commonwealth. The UK has a constitutional monarchy. This means that the king or queen does not rule the country but appoints the government, which the people have chosen in a democratic election.

The monarch invites the leader of the party with the largest number of MPs or the leader of a coalition between more than one party, to become the Prime Minister. The monarch has regular meetings with the Prime Minister and can advise, warn and encourage, but the decisions on government policies are made by the Prime Minister and cabinet

The Queen has reigned since her father's death in 1952, and in 2012 she celebrated her Diamond Jubilee (60 years as queen). She is married to Prince Philip, the Duke of Edinburgh. Her eldest son, Prince Charles (the Prince of Wales), is the heir to the throne.

The Queen has important ceremonial roles, such as the opening of the new parliamentary session each year. On this occasion the Queen makes a speech which summarises the government's policies for the year ahead. All Acts of Parliament are made in her name.

The National Anthem
The National Anthem of the UK is 'God Save the Queen'. It is played at important national occasions and at events attended by the Queen or the Royal Family. The first verse is:

'God save our gracious Queen!
Long live our noble Queen!
God save the Queen!
Send her victorious,
Happy and glorious,
Long to reign over us,
God save the Queen!'

New citizens swear or affirm loyalty to the Queen as part of the citizenship ceremony.

New citizens swear or affirm loyalty to the Queen as part of the citizenship ceremony.

Oath of allegiance
I (name) swear by Almighty God that on becoming a British citizen, I will be faithful and bear true allegiance to Her Majesty Queen Elizabeth the Second, her Heirs and Successors, according to law.

Affirmation of allegiance
I (name) do solemnly, sincerely and truly declare and affirm that on becoming a British citizen, I will be faithful and bear true allegiance to Her Majesty Queen Elizabeth the Second, her Heirs and Successors, according to law.

The system of government in the UK is a parliamentary democracy. The UK is divided into parliamentary constituencies. Voters in each constituency elect their Member of Parliament (MP) in a General Election. All of the elected MPs form the House of Commons. Most MPs belong to a political party, and the party with the majority of MPs forms the government. If one party does not get a majority, two parties can join together to form a coalition.

The House of Commons

The House of Commons is regarded as the more important of the two chambers in Parliament because its members are democratically elected. The Prime Minister and almost all the members of the cabinet are members of the House of Commons (MPs). Each MP represents a parliamentary constituency, which is a small area of the country. MPs have a number of different responsibilities. They:

- Represent everyone in their constituency
- Help to create new laws
- Scrutinize and comment on what the government is doing
- Debate important national issues

Members of the House of Lords, known as peers, are not elected by the people and do not represent a constituency. The role and membership of the House of Lords has changed over the last 50 years. Until 1958, all peers were:
• 'hereditary', which means they inherited their title, or
• senior judges, or
• bishops of the Church of England.
Life peers are appointed by the monarch on the advice of the Prime Minister. Since 1999, hereditary peers have lost the automatic right to attend the House of Lords. They now elect a few of their number to represent them in the House of Lords.

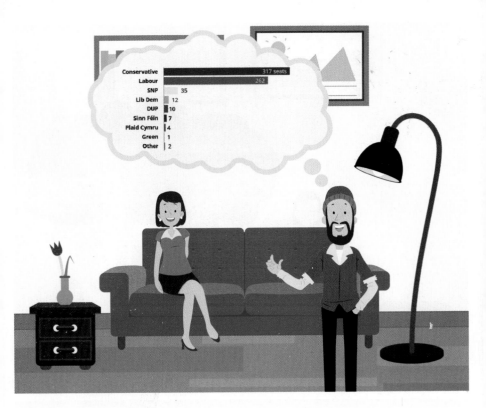

MPs are elected at a General Election, which is held at least every five years. If an MP dies or resigns, there will be a fresh election, called a by-election, in his or her constituency.

MPs are elected through a system called 'first past the post'. In each constituency, the candidate who gets the most votes is elected. The government is usually formed by the party that wins the majority of constituencies. If no party wins a majority, two parties may join together to form a coalition.

Elections for the European Parliament are also held every five years. Elected members are called members of the European Parliament (MEPs). Elections to the European Parliament use a system of proportional representation, where seats are allocated to each party in proportion to the total number of votes it has won.

All elected members have a duty to serve and represent their constituents. You can get contact details for all your representatives and their parties from your local library and from www.parliament.uk. MPs, Assembly members, members of the Scottish Parliament (MSPs) and MEPs are also listed in The Phone Book, published by BT, and in Yellow Pages.

You can contact MPs by letter or telephone at their constituency office, or at their office in the House of Commons: The House of Commons, Westminster, London SW1A OAA, telephone 0207729 3000. In addition, many MPs, Assembly members, MSPs and MEPs hold regular local 'surgeries', where constituents can go in person to talk about issues that are of concern to them. These surgeries are often advertised in the local newspaper.

Debates in the House of Commons are chaired by the Speaker. This person is the chief officer of the House of Commons. The Speaker is neutral and does not represent a political party, even though he or she is an MP, represents a constituency and deals with the constituents' problems like any other MP. The Speaker is chosen by other MPs in a secret ballot.

The Speaker keeps order during political debates to make sure the rules are followed. This includes making sure the opposition (see the section on 'The government') has a guaranteed amount of time to debate issues which it chooses. The Speaker also represents Parliament on ceremonial occasions.

The official home of the Prime Minister is 10 Downing Street, in central London, near the Houses of Parliament.

He or she also has a country house outside London called Chequers. The Prime Minister can be changed if the MPs in the governing party decide to do so, or if he or she wishes to resign. The Prime Minister usually resigns if his or her party loses a General Election.

The Prime Minister appoints about 20 senior MPs to become ministers in charge of departments. These include:
• Chancellor of the Exchequer – responsible for the economy
• Home Secretary – responsible for crime, policing and immigration
• Foreign Secretary - responsible for managing relationships with foreign countries
• Other ministers (called 'Secretaries of State') responsible for subjects such as education, health and defence.

These ministers form the cabinet, a committee which usually meets weekly and makes important decisions about government policy. Many of the decisions have to be debated or approved by Parliament.

Each department also has a number of other ministers, called Ministers of State and Parliamentary Under-Secretaries of State, who take charge of particular areas of the department's work.

The leader of the opposition also appoints senior opposition MPs to be 'shadow ministers'. They form the shadow cabinet and their role is to challenge the government and put forward alternative policies.
There are a few MPs who do not represent any of the main political parties. They are called 'independents' and usually represent an issue important to their constituency.

Pressure and lobby groups are organisations which try to influence government policy. They play an important role in politics. Some are representative organisations such as the CBI (Confederation of British Industry), which represents the views of British business. Others campaign on particular topics, such as the environment (for example, Greenpeace) or human rights (for example, Liberty).

Civil servants support the government in developing and implementing its policies. They also deliver public services. Civil servants are accountable to ministers. They are chosen on merit and are politically neutral – they are not political appointees. People can apply to join the civil service through an application process, like other jobs in the UK. Civil servants are expected to carry out their role with dedication and a commitment to the civil service and its core values. These are: integrity, honesty, objectivity and impartiality (including being politically neutral).

Towns, cities and rural areas in the UK are governed by democratically elected councils, often called 'local authorities'. Some areas have both district and county councils, which have different functions. Most large towns and cities have a single local authority.

London has 33 local authorities, with the Greater London Authority and the Mayor of London coordinating policies across the capital. Many local authorities appoint a mayor, who is the ceremonial leader of the council. In some towns, a mayor is elected to be the effective leader of the administration.

Since 1997, some powers have been devolved from the central government to give people in Wales, Scotland and Northern Ireland more control over matters that directly affect them. These powers are known as devolved administrations.

The Welsh government and National Assembly for Wales are based in Cardiff, the capital city of Wales. The National Assembly has 60 Assembly members (AMs) and elections are held every four years using a form of proportional representation. Members can speak in either Welsh or English, and all of the Assembly's publications are in both languages.

The Assembly has the power to make laws for Wales in 20 areas, including:
• education and training
• health and social services
• economic development
• housing.
Since 2011, the National Assembly for Wales has been able to pass laws on these topics without the agreement of the UK Parliament.
In Wales the elected members, known as Am's meet in the Welsh Assembly in the Senedd in Cardiff Bay (for more information, see www.wales.gov.uk)

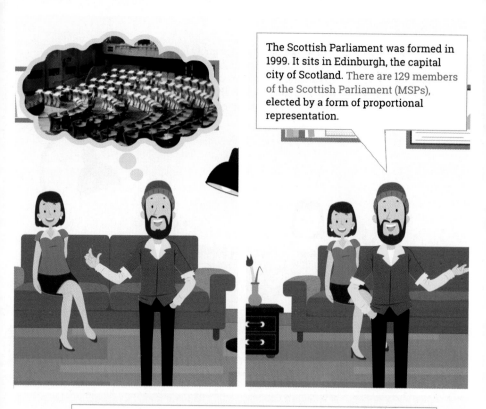

The Scottish Parliament was formed in 1999. It sits in Edinburgh, the capital city of Scotland. There are 129 members of the Scottish Parliament (MSPs), elected by a form of proportional representation.

The Scottish Parliament can pass laws for Scotland of all matters which are not specifically reserved to the UK Parliament. The matters on which the Scottish Parliament can legislate include: Civil and criminal law, Health, Education, Planning & Additional tax-raising powers.
In Scotland the elected members, called MSPs, meet in the Scottish Parliament building at Holyrood in Edinburgh (for more information, see www.scottish.parliament.uk).

A Northern Ireland Parliament was established in 1922, when Ireland was divided, but it was abolished in 1972, shortly after the Troubles broke out in 1969.

The Northern Ireland Assembly was established soon after the Belfast Agreement (or Good Friday Agreement) in 1998. There is a power-sharing agreement which distributes ministerial offices amongst the main parties. The Assembly has 108 elected members, known as MLAs (members of the Legislative Assembly). They are elected with a form of proportional representation.

The Northern Ireland Assembly can make decisions on issues such as:
• education
• agriculture
• the environment
• health
• social services.

The UK government has the power to suspend all devolved assemblies. It has used this power several times in Northern Ireland when local political leaders found it difficult to work together. However, the Assembly been running successfully since 2007.

The UK has had a fully democratic voting system since 1928. **The present voting age of 18 was set in 1969 and (with a few exceptions) all UK-born and naturalised adult citizens have the right to vote.**

Adult citizens of the UK, and citizens of the Commonwealth and the Irish Republic who are resident in the UK, can vote in all public elections. Adult citizens of other EU states who are resident in the UK can vote in all elections except General Elections.

To be able to vote, you can register by contacting your local council electoral registration office. This is usually based at your local council (in Scotland it may be based elsewhere).

If you don't know which local authority you come under, you can find out by visiting www.aboutmyvote.co.uk and entering you postcode. You can also download voter registration forms in English, Welsh and some other languages. The electoral register is updated every year in September or October. An electoral registration form is sent to every household and this has to be completed and returned with the names of everyone who is resident in the household and eligible to vote.

In Northern Ireland a different system operates. This is called 'individual registration' and all those entitled to vote must complete their own registration form. Once registered, people stay on the register provided their personal details do not change. For more information see the Electoral Office for Northern Ireland website at www.eoni.org.uk

By law, each local authority has to make its electoral register available for anyone to look at, although this has to be supervised. The register is kept at each local electoral registration office (or council office in England and Wales). It is also possible to see the register at some public buildings such as libraries.

People vote in elections at places called polling stations, or polling places in Scotland. Before the election you will be sent a poll card. This tells you where your polling station or polling place is and when the election will take place. On election day, the polling station or place will be open from 7.00 am until 10.00 pm.

When you arrive at the polling station, the staff will ask for your name and address. In Northern Ireland you will also have to show photographic identification. If it is difficult for you to get to a polling station or polling place, you can register for a postal ballot. Your ballot paper will be sent to your home before the election. You then fill it in and post it back. You can choose to do this when you register to vote.

Most citizens of the UK, the Irish republic or the Commonwealth aged 18 or over can stand for public office. There are some exceptions, including:
• Members of the armed forces
• Civil servants
• People found guilty of certain criminal offences.
Members of the House of Lords may not stand for election to the House of Commons but are eligible for all other public offices.

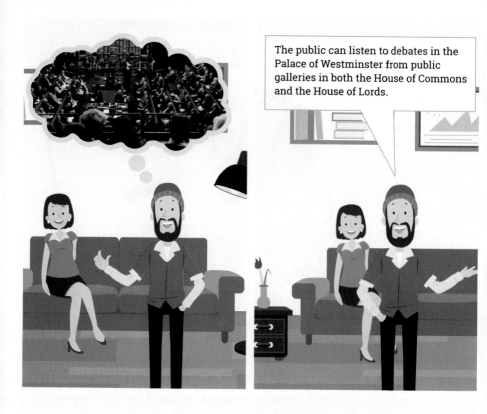

The public can listen to debates in the Palace of Westminster from public galleries in both the House of Commons and the House of Lords.

You can write to your local MP in advance to ask for tickets or you can Queue on the day at the public entrance. Entrance is free. Sometimes there are long queues for the House of Commons and people have to wait for at least one or two hours. It is usually easier to get in to the House of Lords. You can find further information on the UK Parliament website at www.parliament.uk

In Northern Ireland elected members, known as MLAs, meet in the Northern Ireland Assembly at Stormont, in Belfast.
There are two ways to arrange a visit to Stormont. You can either contact the Education Service (details are on the Northern Ireland Assembly website at www.niassembly.gov.uk) or contact an MLA.

In Wales the elected members, known as AMs, meet in the Welsh Assembly in the Senedd in Cardiff Bay (for more information, see www.wales.gov.uk).

The Senedd is an open building. You can book guided tours or seats in the public galleries for the Welsh Assembly. To make a booking, contact the Assembly Booking Service on 0845 010 5500 or email assembly.bookings@wales.gsi.gov.uk

Proceedings in Parliament are broadcast on television and published in official reports called Hansard.

Written reports can be found in large libraries and at www.parliament.uk. Most people get information about political issues and events from newspapers (often called 'the press'), television, radio and the internet. The UK has a free press. This means that what is written in newspapers is free from government control. Some newspaper owners and editors hold strong political opinions and run campaigns to try to influence government policy and public opinion. By law, radio and television coverage of the political parties must be balanced and so equal time has to be given to rival viewpoints.

FLAGS OF THE COMMONWEALTH OF NATIONS

The Commonwealth is an association of countries that support each other and work together towards shared goals in democracy and development. Most member states were once part of the British Empire, although a few countries which were not have also joined.

The Queen is the ceremonial head of the Commonwealth, which currently has 54 member states (see table below). Membership is voluntary. The Commonwealth has no power over its members, although it can suspend membership. The Commonwealth is based on the core values of democracy, good government and the rule of law.

Commonwealth members		
Antigua and Barbuda	Australia	The Bahamas
Bangladesh	Barbados	Belize
Botswana	Brunei Darussalam	Cameroon
Canada	Cyprus	Dominica
Fiji (currently suspended)	The Gambia	Ghana
Grenada	Guyana	India
Jamaica	Kenya	Kiribati
Lesotho	Malawi	Malaysia
Maldives	Malta	Mauritius
Mozambique	Namibia	Nauru
New Zealand	Nigeria	Pakistan
Papua New Guinea	Rwanda	Samoa
Seychelles	Sierra Leone	Singapore
Solomon Islands	South Africa	Sri Lanka
St Kitts and Nevis	St Lucia	St Vincent and the Grenadines
Swaziland	Tanzania	Tonga
Trinidad and Tobago	Tuvalu	Uganda
UK	Vanuatu	Zambia

The European Union

The European Union (EU), originally called the European Economic Community (EEC), was set up by six western European countries (Belgium, France, Germany, Italy, Luxembourg and the Netherlands) who signed the Treaty of Rome on 25 March 1957. The UK originally decided not to join this group but it became a member in 1973. There are now 27 EU member states (see table below). Croatia will also become a member state in 2013.

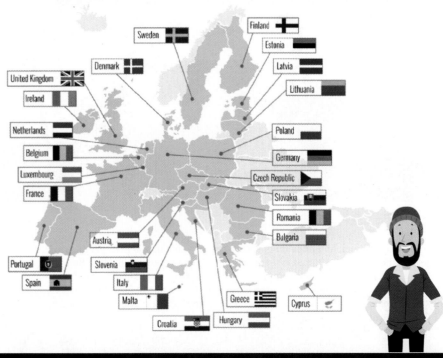

EU member states		
Austria	Belgium	Bulgaria
Cyprus	Czech Republic	Denmark
Estonia	Finland	France
Germany	Greece	Hungary
Ireland	Italy	Latvia
Lithuania	Luxembourg	Malta
Netherlands	Poland	Portugal
Romania	Slovakia	Slovenia
Spain	Sweden	UK

EU law is legally binding in the UK and all the EU member states. European laws are called directives, regulations or framework decisions.

The Council of Europe is separate from the EU. It has 47 member countries, including the UK, and is responsible for the protection and promotion of human rights in those countries. It has no power to make laws but draws up conventions and charters, the most well-known of which is the European Convention on Human Rights and Fundamental Freedoms, usually called the European Convention on Human Rights.

The UK is part of the United Nations (UN), an international organization with more than 190 countries as members.
The UN was set up after the Second World War and aims to prevent war and promote international peace and security. There are 15 members on the UN Security Council, which recommends action when there are international crises and threats to peace. The UK is one of five permanent members of the Security Council.

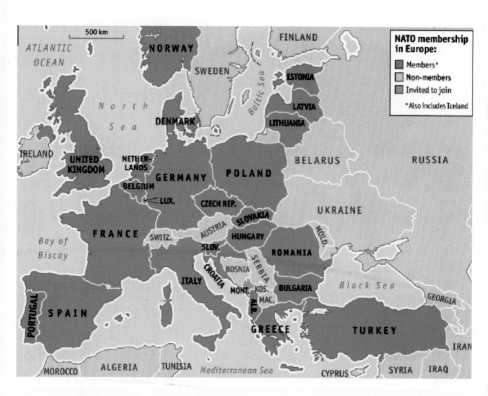

The North Atlantic Treaty Organization (NATO)
The UK is also a member of NATO. NATO is a group of European and North American countries that have agreed to help each other if they come under attack. It also aims to maintain peace between all of its members.

Britain is proud of being a welcoming country, but all residents, regardless of their background, are expected to comply with the law and to understand that some things which may be allowed in other legal systems are not acceptable in the UK.

The law is relevant to all areas of life in the UK. You should make sure that you are aware of the laws which affect your everyday life, including both your personal and business affairs.

Every person in the UK receives equal treatment under the law. This means that the law applies in the same way to everyone, no matter who they are or where they are from.
Laws can be divided into criminal law and civil law:

Criminal law relates to crimes, which are usually investigated by the police or another authority such as a council, and which are punished by the courts.

Civil law is used to settle disputes between individuals or groups.

Examples of criminal laws are:

- Carrying a weapon: it is a criminal offence to carry a weapon of any kind, **even if it is for self-defence. This includes a gun, a knife or anything that is made or adapted to cause injury.**

- Drugs: selling or buying drugs such as heroin, cocaine, ecstasy and cannabis is illegal in the UK.

- Racial crime: it is a criminal offence to cause harassment, alarm or distress to someone because of their religion or ethnic origin.

- Selling tobacco: it is illegal to sell tobacco products (for example, cigarettes, cigars, roll-up tobacco) to anyone under the age of 18.

- Smoking in public places: it is against the law to smoke tobacco products in nearly every enclosed public place in the UK. There are signs displayed to tell you where you cannot smoke.

- Buying alcohol: it is a criminal offence to sell alcohol to anyone who is under 18 or to buy alcohol for people who are under the age of 18. **(There is one exception: people aged 16 or over can drink alcohol with a meal in a hotel or restaurant)**

- Drinking in public: some places have alcohol-free zones where you cannot drink in public. The police can also confiscate alcohol or move young people on from public places. You can be fined or arrested.

Examples of civil laws are:

* Housing law: this includes disputes between landlords and tenants over issues suck as repairs and eviction.

* Consumer rights: an example of this is a dispute about faulty goods or services.

* Employment law: these cases include disputes over wages and cases of unfair dismissal or discrimination in the workplace.

* Debt: people might be taken to court if they owe money to someone.

The police and their duties

The job of the police in the UK is to:
• Protect life and property
• Prevent disturbances
• Prevent and detect crime.

The police are organised into a number of separate police forces headed by Chief Constables. They are independent of the government.

Anyone can make a complaint about the police by going to a police station and writing to the Chief Constable of the police force involved. In November 2012, the public elected Police and Crime Commissioners (PCCs) in England and Wales. These are directly elected individuals who are responsible for the delivery of an efficient and effective police force that reflects the needs of their local communities. PCCs set local police priorities and the local policing budget. They also appoint the local Chief Constable.

The UK faces a range of terrorist threats. The most serious of these is from Al Qa'ida, its affiliates and like-minded organisations. The UK also faces threats from other kind of terrorism, such as Northern Ireland-related terrorism.

Judges (who are together called 'the judiciary') are responsible for interpreting the law and ensuring that trials are conducted fairly. The government cannot interfere with this.

Criminal courts
There are some differences between the court systems in England and Wales, Scotland and Northern Ireland.

In England, Wales and Northern Ireland, most minor criminal cases are dealt with in a Magistrates' Court. In Scotland, minor criminal offences go to a Justice of the Peace Court.

Magistrates decide the verdict in each case that comes before them and, if the person is found guilty, the sentence that they are given. In Northern Ireland, cases are heard by a District Judge or Deputy District Judge, who is legally qualified and paid.

In England, Wales and Northern Ireland, serious offences are tried in front of a judge and a jury in a Crown Court. In Scotland, serious cases are heard in a Sheriff Court with either a sheriff or a sheriff with a jury. The most serious cases in Scotland, such as murder, are heard at a High Court with a judge and jury. A jury is made up of members of the public chosen at random from the local electoral register.

In England, Wales and Northern Ireland a jury has 12 members, and in Scotland a jury has 15 members. Everyone who is summoned to do jury service must do it unless they are not eligible (for example, because they have a criminal conviction) or they provide a good reason to be excused, such as ill health.

The jury has to listen to the evidence presented at the trial and then decide a verdict of 'guilty' or 'not guilty' based of what they have heard. In Scotland, a third verdict of 'not proven' is also possible. If the jury finds a defendant guilty, the judge decides the penalty.

In England, Wales and Northern Ireland, if an accused person is aged 10 to 17, the case is normally heard in a Youth Court in front of up to three specially trained magistrates or a District Judge. The most serious cases will go to the Crown Court. The parents or carers of the young person are expected to attend the hearing.

Members of the public are not allowed in Youth Courts, and the name or photographs of the accused young person cannot be published in newspapers or used by the media.

In Scotland a system called the Children's Hearings System is used to deal with children and young people who have committed an offence.

Northern Ireland has a system of youth conferencing to consider how a child should be dealt with when they have committed an offence.

County Courts

County Courts deal with a wide range of civil disputes. These include people trying to get back money that is owed to them, cases involving personal injury, family matters, breaches of contract, and divorce. In Scotland, most of these matters are dealt with in the Sheriff Court. More serious civil cases – for example, when a large amount of compensation is being claimed – are dealt with in the High Court of England, Wales and Northern Ireland. In Scotland, they are dealt with in the Court of Session in Edinburgh.

In England, Wales and Northern Ireland, serious offences are tried in front of a judge and a jury in a Crown Court. In Scotland, serious cases are heard in a Sheriff Court with either a sheriff or a sheriff with a jury. The most serious cases in Scotland, such as murder, are heard at a High Court with a judge and jury. A jury is made up of members of the public chosen at random from the local electoral register.

The small claims procedure is an informal way of helping people to settle minor disputes without spending a lot of time and money using a lawyer. This procedure is used for claims of less than £5,000 in England and Wales and £3,000 in Scotland and Northern Ireland. The hearing is held in front of a judge in an ordinary room, and people from both sides of the dispute sit around a table. Small claims can also be issued online through Money Claims Online (www.moneyclaim.gov.uk).

You can get details about the small claims procedure from your local County Court or Sheriff Court. Details of your local court can be found as follows:
• England and Wales: at www.gov.uk
• Scotland: at www.scotcourts.gov.uk
• Northern Ireland: at www.courtsni.gov.uk

Solicitors are trained lawyers who give advice on legal matters, take action for their clients and represent their clients in court. There are solicitors' offices throughout the UK. It is important to find out which aspects of law a solicitor specialises in and to check that they have the right experience to help you with your case. Many advertise in local newspapers and in Yellow Pages.

Solicitors Regulation Authority

The Citizens Advice Bureau (www.citizensadvice.org.uk) can give you names of local solicitors and which areas of law they specialise in. You can also get this information from the Law Society (www.lawsociety.org.uk) in England and Wales

The Law Society of Scotland (www.lawscot.org.uk) or the Law Society of Northern Ireland (www.lawsoc-ni.org). Solicitors' charges are usually based on how much time they spend of a case. It is very important to find out at the start how much a case is likely to cost.

Fundamental Principles

Britain has a long history of respecting an individual's rights and ensuring essential freedoms. These rights have their roots in Magna Carta, the Habeas Corpus Act and the Bill of Rights of 1689, and they have developed over a period of time. British diplomats and lawyers had an important role in drafting the European Convention on Human Rights and Fundamental Freedoms. The UK was one of the first countries to sign the Convention in 1950.

Some of the principles included in the European Convention of Human Rights are:
- right to life
- prohibition of torture
- prohibition of slavery and forced labour
- right to liberty and security
- right to a fair trial
- freedom of thought, conscience and religion
- freedom of expression (speech).

The Human Rights Act 1998 incorporated the European Convention of Human Rights into UK law. The government, public bodies and the courts must follow the principles of the Convention.

1 THE STATE'S OBLIGATION TO RESPECT HUMAN RIGHTS

2 RIGHT TO LIFE

3 RIGHT NOT TO BE TORTURED

4 RIGHT NOT TO BE ENSLAVED

5 RIGHT TO NOT BE UNLAWFULLY DETAINED

6 RIGHT TO A FAIR TRIAL

7 NO PUNISHMENT WITHOUT LAW

UK laws ensure that people are not treated unfairly in any area of life or work because of their age, disability, sex, pregnancy and maternity, race, religion or belief, sexuality or marital status.

If you face problems with discrimination, you can get more information from the Citizens Advice Bureau or from one of the following organisations:
• England and Wales: Equality and Human Rights Commission (www.equalityhumanrights.com)

• Scotland: Equality and Human Rights Commission in Scotland (www.equalityhumanrights.com/scotland/the-commission-in-scotland) and Scottish Human Rights Commission (www.scottishhumanrights.com)
• Northern Ireland: equality Commission for Northern Ireland (www.equalityni.org)
• Northern Ireland Human Rights Commission (www.nihrc.org).

In the UK, brutality and violence in the home is a serious crime. Anyone who is violent towards their partner – whether they are a man or a woman, married or living together – can be prosecuted. Any man who forces a woman to have sex, including a woman's husband, can be charged with rape. It is important for anyone facing domestic violence to get help as soon as possible. A solicitor or the Citizens Advice Bureau can explain the available options. In some areas there are safe places to go and stay in, called refuges or shelters.

There are emergency telephone numbers in the helpline section at the front of Yellow Pages, including, for women, the number of the nearest women's centre. You can also phone the 24-hour National Domestic Violence Freephone Helpline on 0808 2000 247 at any time, or the police can help you find a safe place to stay.

Female genital mutilation
Female genital mutilation (FGM), also known as cutting or female circumcision, is illegal in the UK. Practicing FGM or taking a girl or woman abroad for FGM is a criminal offence.

A marriage should be entered into with the full and free consent of both people involved. Arranged marriages, where both parties agree to the marriage, are acceptable in the UK.

Forced marriage is where one or both parties do not or cannot give their consent to enter into the partnership. Forcing another person to marry is a criminal offence.
Forced Marriage Protection Orders were introduced in 2008 for England, Wales and Northern Ireland under the Forced Marriage (Civil Protection) Act 2007.

Court orders can be obtained to protect a person from being forced into a marriage, or to protect a person in a forced marriage. Similar Protection Orders were introduced in Scotland in November 2011. A potential victim, or someone acting for them, can apply for an order. Anyone found to have breached an order can be jailed for up to two years for contempt of court.

Income tax
People in the UK have to pay tax on their income, which includes: Wages from paid employment, Profits from self-employment, Taxable benefits, Pensions and Income from property, savings and dividends. Money raised from income tax pays for government services such as roads, education, police and the armed forces.

HMRC
HM Revenue & Customs

For most people, the right amount of income tax is automatically taken from their income from employment by their employer and paid directly to HM Revenue & Customs (HMRC), the government department that collects taxes. This system is called "Pay As You Earn" (PAYE). If you are self-employed, you need to pay your own tax through a system called 'self-assessment', which includes completing a tax return. Other people may also need to complete a tax return. If HMRC sends you a tax return, it is important to complete and return the form as soon as you have all the necessary information.

You can find out more about income tax at www.hmrc.gov.uk/incometax. You can get help and advice about taxes and completing tax forms from the HMRC self-assessment helpline, on 0845 300 0627, and the HMRC website at www.hmrc.gov.uk

Almost everybody in the UK who is in paid work, including self-employed people, must pay National Insurance Contributions. The money raised from National Insurance Contributions is used to pay for state benefits and services such as the state retirement pension and the National Health Service (NHS).

Employees have their National Insurance Contributions deducted from their pay by their employer. People who are self-employed need to pay National Insurance Contributions themselves.
Anyone who does not pay enough National Insurance Contributions will not be able to receive certain contributory benefits such as Jobseeker's Allowance or a full state retirement pension.

Some workers, such as part-time workers,
may not qualify for statutory payments such as maternity pay if they do not earn enough.
Further guidance about National Insurance Contributions is available on HMRC's website at www.hmrc.gov.uk/ni

In the UK, you must be at least 17 years to drive a car or motor cycle and you must have a driving licence to drive on public roads. To get a UK driving licence you must pass a driving test, which tests both your knowledge and your practical skills. You need to be at least 16 years old to ride a moped, and there are other age requirements and special tests for driving large vehicles.

Drivers can use their driving licence until they are 70 years old. After that, the licence is valid for three years at a time.

In Northern Ireland, a newly qualified driver must display an 'R' plate (for restricted driver) for one year after passing the test.

If your driving licence if from a country in the European Union (EU), Iceland, Liechtenstein or Norway, you can drive in the UK for as long as your licence is valid. If you have a licence from any other country, you may use it in the UK for up to 12 months. To continue driving after that, you must get a UK full driving licence.

If you are resident in the UK, your car or motor cycle must be registered at the Driver and Vehicle Licensing Agency (DVLA). You must pay an annual road tax and display the tax disc, which shows that the tax has been paid, on the windowscreen. You must also have valid motor insurance. It is a serious criminal offence to drive without insurance. If your vehicle is over three years old, you must take it to the Ministry of Transport (MOT) test every year. It is an offense not to have a MOT certificate if your vehicle is more than three years old. You can find out more about vehicle tax and MOT requirements from www.gov.uk

Your role in the community

Becoming a British citizen or settling in the UK brings responsibilities but also opportunities. Everyone has the opportunity to participate in their community. This section looks at some of the responsibilities of being a citizen and gives information about how you can help to make your community a better place to live and work.

Values and responsibilities

Although Britain is one of the world's most diverse societies, there is a set of shared values and responsibilities that everyone can agree with. These values and responsibilities include:

• To obey and respect the law
• To be aware of the rights of others and respect those rights
• To treat others with fairness
• To behave responsibly
• To help and protect your family
• To respect and preserve the environment
• To treat everyone equally, regardless of sex, race, religion, age, disability, class or sexual orientation
• To work to provide for yourself and your family
• To help others
• To vote in local and national government elections.

Taking on these values and responsibilities will make it easier for you to become a full and active citizen.

As well as getting the right to vote, people on the electoral register are randomly selected to serve on a jury. Anyone who is on the electoral register and is aged 18 to 70 can be asked to do this.
Everyone who is summoned to do jury service must do it unless they are not eligible (for example, because they have a criminal conviction) or they provide a good reason to be excused, such as ill health.

School governors, or members of the school board in Scotland, are people from the local community who wish to make a positive contribution to their children's education. They must be aged 18 or over at the date of their election or appointment. There is no upper age limit.

Governors and school boards have an important part to play in raising school standards. They have three key roles:
• Setting the strategic direction of the school
• Ensuring accountability
• Monitoring and evaluating school performance.

Political parties are particularly busy at election times. Members work hard to persuade people to vote for their candidates – for instance, by handing out leaflets in the street or by knocking on people's doors and asking for their support. This is called 'canvassing'.

Donated blood is used by hospitals to help people with a wide range of injuries and illnesses. Giving blood only takes about an hour to do.